10

Career
Essentials

Para un trabajo 10...
¡muéstrales lo mejor de tí!
16.05.11   Paloma

10
Career Essentials

. . . .

Excel at Your Career
By Using Your Personality Type

Donna Dunning

NICHOLAS BREALEY
PUBLISHING

BOSTON · LONDON

First published by Nicholas Brealey Publishing in 2010.

20 Park Plaza, Suite 1115A
Boston, MA 02116, USA
Tel: + 617-523-3801
Fax: + 617-523-3708

3-5 Spafield Street, Clerkenwell
London, EC1R 4QB, UK
Tel: +44-(0)-207-239-0360
Fax: +44-(0)-207-239-0370

www.nicholasbrealey.com

Myers-Briggs Type Indicator® and MBTI® are trademarks or registered trademarks of the Myers-Briggs Type Indicator Trust in the United States and other countries.

Printed in the United States of America

14 13 12 11 10   1 2 3 4 5

ISBN: 978-1-85788-542-2

Library of Congress Cataloging-in-Publication Data
Dunning, Donna, 1955–
    10 career essentials : Excel at your career by using your personality type
Donna Dunning.
        p. cm.
    Includes bibliographical references and index.
    ISBN 978-1-85788-542-2
    1. Career development.   2. Personality and occupation.   I. Title.   II. Title: Ten career
essentials.
    HF5381.D86 2010
    650.1—dc22

                                                                            2010008493

Table of Contents

. . . .

CHAPTER ONE

Introduction

Work is a central part of our lives, with an enormous influence on our lifestyle and personal satisfaction. If you work full time for 40 years, you will spend more than 80,000 hours on the job. Since it consumes a significant part of your life, your career should be interesting, motivating, and rewarding.

There are books that teach you how to paint with watercolors, bake gourmet food, or fix a bicycle, but few that show you how to build career success. That's where this book comes in.

In the following chapters, you will learn the ten essential career success strategies. Each chapter describes one of these essential strategies and provides self-assessment tools, questions, and tips to stimulate your understanding. Mastering the essentials is key to your career success.

The Ten Essential Career Success Strategies

1. Ask yourself for directions

Career success means something different to everyone. It occurs when your career direction aligns with who you are and what is important to you. To build a successful career, you need to determine what success looks like for *you*. After you define success, you can set and meet your personal career and life goals. When you master this success strategy, you channel your efforts in the right direction to ensure that your career brings you personal and professional satisfaction.

2. Optimize your outlook

People quickly judge you based on what you do and say and how you look, walk, and talk. When you take care of yourself, manage stress, and demonstrate a positive attitude and confidence, people enjoy interacting with you and value your contribution. Optimizing your outlook improves both your health and your career success. When you have a positive attitude and believe in and take care of yourself, you can reach your goals more easily.

3. Put yourself in charge

When you put yourself in charge of your career, you take ownership of your mistakes and accomplishments. You stand behind what you say and do. When you take responsibility for your words and actions, you link your efforts to success and learn from your mistakes. Others count on you and see you as determined, dependable, reliable, and dedicated, all qualities much needed and rewarded in the workforce.

4. Learn from everyone

Everyone can teach you something. To be successful, you need to pay attention to what others have to say. You benefit when you listen carefully, gain a clear understanding of others' expectations, and respond positively to feedback. When you strive to learn from anyone, you begin to embrace multiple perspectives, benefit from corrective feedback, and develop rapport. If you are open to, and eager to learn from, others, many opportunities will come your way.

5. Relate to anyone

Your career success depends on your ability to express yourself clearly, directly, and diplomatically. When you share your perspectives and provide information and constructive feedback, you leave little room for miscommunication or misunderstanding. When you relate to everyone, you resolve conflicts and problems so that everyone benefits. You accomplish your goals by working cooperatively. Mastering this career success strategy provides you with a network of contacts willing to support your career development.

6. Cultivate your curiosity

Our information- and Internet-focused age offers a wealth of facts and ideas. When you cultivate your curiosity, you manage the large amounts of information available and become a lifelong learner. You are interested, up-to-date, knowledgeable, and aware. You use what you learn to help you work more effectively. You understand your learning style and use learning strategies to retain important information. Others are confident in your ability to learn new skills and apply new information, and they will think of you when opportunities or challenges arise.

7. Disentangle your thoughts

To be successful at work, you need to hone and direct your thinking to deal with the situation at hand. When you disentangle your thoughts, you can consider and then select the right approach, strategies, and tools for making decisions and tackling tasks and problems. You make well-thought-out decisions and solve problems effectively. Others see you as resourceful and strategic. You use a flexible combination of thinking modes: practical, creative, global, logical, and humanistic.

8. Exceed expectations

Others need to know they can count on you to achieve exceptional results. To exceed expectations, you must prioritize, plan, organize your time and activities, and persist. When you work to a high standard and continuously look for ways to improve your work, people see you as results oriented, productive, persistent, efficient, and effective. When you show pride in your work and take initiative, others know you will do a good job, and they feel confident offering you new and important tasks and projects.

9. Thrive in uncertainty

Those who are successful in their careers accept that the world is changing rapidly. To thrive in uncertainty, you need to take a heads-up approach to work, observing patterns and trends and anticipating change so you can quickly adjust. When you thrive in uncertainty, you make the most of opportunities by being adaptable and proactive, and you position yourself for success. Others see you as flexible and versatile, and they are confident in your ability to cope with unexpected changes.

10. **Promote your progress**

To create your success, you need to let others know your goals and aspirations so they can assist and guide your progress. You can also promote your skills, interests, experience, and other valuable personal qualities. Self-promotion opens the door to opportunities by showing people who you are and what you can do.

How to Use This Book

The starting point for your career development is self-awareness. Each chapter in this book stimulates your thinking and encourages you to identify your unique learning needs. Only you can decide which of the essential career success strategies you already use well and which you need to develop. Each chapter contains self-assessment tools. These tools help you identify and make the most of your strengths, and highlight potential areas for development. Each chapter also provides tips for optimizing the career success strategy.

Chapter 2 introduces personality type as a tool for customizing your learning. Personality type can help you understand your personal learning style and work preferences. Personality type tips in each chapter show you how to tailor the career success strategies to your personal preferences.

To get the most from this book, *interact*. Complete the self-assessment exercises, think about and answer the questions, and use the reflection and action exercise at the end of each chapter to set personal goals. Each career strategy is linked to concrete behaviors you can learn. Take control by choosing behaviors you want to change. Only you can create your ideal career path.

Self-assessment is not always easy. Ask for feedback from those willing to support your learning. They may be able to help you target areas for improvement and growth. They also can encourage and assist your efforts as you strive to improve.

This book is designed to help you create career satisfaction and success on your own terms. Enjoy your journey.

CHAPTER TWO

· ·

Ask Yourself for Directions

Career success is commonly measured by money, power, and prestige. However, these are not the only sources of work satisfaction. Only you can define what your career success looks like. You have a unique combination of interests, skills, values, and personality preferences. You are in a specific situation, faced with your own set of constraints, and in search of a suitable lifestyle. This chapter will help you identify your personal approach to work and clearly define your career goals and aspirations.

When you use your natural preferences and strengths every day, work becomes more interesting and rewarding. Knowing your personality preferences can help you decide what your own career success will look like. Personality type, based on the work of Carl Jung, identifies your natural preferences and strengths. You can use personality type to figure out how you prefer to do your work. When you know how you prefer to work and what kind of work you prefer to do, you can choose the right career direction and focus your energy on career success.

Jung's theory of personality type has been expanded and popularized through the work of Katharine Cook Briggs and Isabel Briggs Myers. This mother-daughter team created the Myers-Briggs Type Indicator® (MBTI®) personality inventory, a nonjudgmental assessment tool for identifying personality type that has thrived through more than 60 years of research and development.

· ·

This chapter will help you identify your natural personality preferences and provide strategies for clarifying your life and career goals. It is not designed to help you choose a career or change careers. Rather, it is designed to help you hone your existing career and life goals. If you are unsure of your career direction, you may want to engage in a more complete career-planning process, such as that described in the companion book *What's Your Type of Career?*

10 Career Essentials provides you with a review of the personality type preferences assessed by the MBTI® instrument and an informal way to self-assess your preferences. By reading the descriptions and filling in the check boxes on the next pages you will start to discover your natural personality preferences. It is important to note that the descriptions given here are general, so not all statements will apply to you or any other specific individual.

The preferences you express and develop are greatly influenced by your current situation and past experiences. There are many personal and situational factors that may influence how you see yourself. You may have ignored your natural disposition and learned the skills and attributes of an opposing preference in order to be successful. You may be at a point in your life where you need to or choose to develop preferences you have not used much in the past. Others may be encouraging or pressuring you to demonstrate behaviors that don't align with the way you naturally would prefer to act. For these reasons, a single checklist may not provide enough information for you to sort out what is learned and expected from what is natural for you.

To most accurately identify your natural preferences it is best to complete the official MBTI® instrument. The Association for Psychological Type International (APTi) can refer you to a specialist in your area who can administer and interpret the MBTI® personality assessment. The URL for the APTi website is www.aptinternational.org. You can also take the official MBTI® personality assessment online at www.mbticomplete.com. This online version of the personality assessment guides you through an interpretation process to validate your personality preferences.

In personality type theory, the characteristic ways in which you prefer to function and orient yourself to the world are grouped into four pairs. You will naturally prefer one element of each pair to the other. By choosing one preference from each pair, you can discover a four-letter personality type, one of sixteen possible personality types. Read through the preference pairs on the following pages to identify your personality type preferences, and check the box that best applies to you.

Extraversion and Introversion

Extraversion and Introversion are alternative ways of orienting yourself to the world. Extraversion (E) is an external, active orientation, and Introversion (I) is an internal, reflective orientation.

E: Extraversion   "Let's talk this over."

People who prefer Extraversion tend to

- Focus their energy and process information externally by talking and acting
- Dislike complicated procedures and working on one thing for a long time, especially if they must do so alone
- Learn and work best when able to share, discuss, and process information with others
- Ask questions and think out loud during activities or while working through a decision
- Understand their world best by taking action or talking about it

I: Introversion   "I need to think about this."

People who prefer Introversion tend to

- Focus their energy and process information internally, through reflection and introspection
- Prefer quiet places to work and work contentedly on one thing for a long time
- Learn and work best by having time to understand, and process information on their own
- Think before speaking or acting; they may be uncomfortable when asked to perform or respond on demand
- Downplay their strengths outwardly; as a result, others may underestimate their abilities

Everyone uses Extraversion and Introversion to carry out day-to-day activities. However, one of the two is more natural and comfortable. Check the preference that seems to reflect your personality:

☐ **E: Extraversion**    **I: Introversion**

Sensing and Intuition

Sensing and Intuition are two ways to take in information. Sensing (S) indicates a preference for focusing on specific facts and details. Intuition (N) indicates a preference for focusing on general patterns and possibilities.

S: Sensing   "Just the facts, please."

People who prefer Sensing as a way to take in information tend to

- Focus on individual facts and details before seeing underlying patterns or whole concepts
- Take more interest in the facts as they are known now
- Prefer information and tasks that are presented in a practical, sequential format
- Work at a steady pace
- Become impatient or frustrated with complicated or future-oriented tasks that may take a long time to complete
- Like having their senses engaged at work

N: Intuition   "I can see it all now."

People who prefer Intuition as a way of taking in information tend to

- Focus on what facts mean and how they fit together; they pay more attention to big-picture implications and relationships between ideas than to facts and details alone
- Generate and recognize possibilities and are less interested in realities and data
- Like developing new ideas; are apt to be easily bored with routines and sequential tasks
- Jump around between ideas and tasks at work and in learning activities; they are likely to have bursts of energy rather than stamina

Everyone uses both Sensing and Intuition to carry out day-to-day activities. However, one of the two is more natural and comfortable. Check the preference that seems to reflect your personality:

□ **S: Sensing**   ☑ **N: Intuition**

Thinking and Feeling

Thinking and Feeling describe information processing and decision-making preferences. An individual with a preference for Thinking (T) trusts logic and analysis. An individual who prefers Feeling (F) puts more trust in values and personal consequences.

T: Thinking   "Is this logical?"

People who prefer Thinking as a way to make decisions and process information tend to

- Focus on logic and analysis
- Deal most easily with objective data and cause-and-effect relationships
- Consider the pros and cons of ideas, information, and opinions
- Understand emotions and feelings best when they are introduced as facts and details to consider in decision making and problem solving
- Prefer calm, objective interactions

F: Feeling   "Will anybody be hurt?"

People who prefer Feeling as a way to make decisions and process information tend to

- Take more interest in how information affects people than in the information itself
- Need feedback from other people and work best in an environment that provides support and encouragement
- Consider the atmosphere at work as important as the work itself
- Make subjective decisions; they find it easy to understand and appreciate other people's values
- Find objective, logical reasoning harsh; they may feel criticized by people who function in a logical, analytical mode

Everyone uses both Thinking and Feeling to carry out their day-to-day activities. However, one of the two is more natural and comfortable. Check the preference that seems to reflect your personality:

☐ **T: Thinking**   ☒ **F: Feeling**

Judging and Perceiving

Judging and Perceiving describe two ways of orienting to and dealing with the external world. An individual with a preference for Judging (J) tends to be decisive and prefers structure and control. An individual with a preference for Perceiving (P) tends to keep options open as much as possible and prefers spontaneity and flexibility.

J: Judging   "Just do something."

People who prefer Judging tend to

- Make decisions as soon as possible to have closure
- Plan and organize their world
- Tolerate routines and structure comfortably
- Like roles and expectations to be clear and definite
- Find change and ambiguity uncomfortable
- Complete tasks and move on
- Take an organized approach and have a plan

P: Perceiving   "Let's wait and see."

People who prefer Perceiving tend to

- Defer judgments and gather more information
- Act spontaneously and leave things to the last minute; they may choose not to plan or organize tasks or time
- Prefer starting projects to following through with them
- Stay flexible and adaptable
- Become frustrated by rules, routines, and closure
- Focus on exploring and seeking new information; they embrace change

Everyone uses both Judging and Perceiving to carry out their day-to-day activities. However, one of the two is more natural and comfortable. Check the preference that seems to reflect your personality:

☐ **J: Judging**    **P: Perceiving**

What Are Your Personality Preferences?

Personality type describes your personal preferences for focusing your energy, taking in new information, making decisions, and managing yourself in the world. These preferences are grouped into four pairs. You'll find you naturally prefer one element of each pair over the other. By choosing one preference from each pair, you'll discover which of 16 personality types you belong to.

Confirm Your Personality Preferences

Remember—you use all of the preferences at times, but one of each pair is more natural to you. For example, everyone uses Thinking and Feeling to make decisions; we look at the logical consequences and also consider the needs of those involved in the situation. But you will put more trust in either Thinking or Feeling as you come to a decision.

List the four letters you have chosen as your personality type here:

I N F P

To ensure you have accurately identified your natural preferences, it is best to confirm your four-letter personality type by completing the Myers-Briggs Type Indicator® instrument, a reliable and validated assessment tool administered and interpreted by a trained professional.

What Is Your Natural Way of Working?

The preference pairs have 16 possible combinations. These four-letter personality types are more than the simple sum of the four preferences. Each of the 16 combinations of letters represents a unique way of relating to the world. Although all 16 types are distinct, we can simplify them a bit by placing them in closely related pairs. These pairs of personality types have the same characteristic approach to work, resulting in eight ways of working. The pairs of personality types can be combined because both share their most trusted, comfortable, and developed preference. For example, the ESTP and ESFP personality types both approach the world in a practical, flexible, external, here-and-now way; they are called Responders.

A caveat: Avoid using personality type information to categorize, label, or limit yourself or others. The information only provides general descriptions; not all statements will apply to you or any other individual. For instance, the preferences you express and develop are greatly influenced by your current situation and experiences. You may have ignored your natural disposition and learned the skills and attributes of an opposing preference in your pursuit of success. You may be at a point in your life in which you need, or choose, to develop preferences you haven't used much in the past. The characteristics and descriptors of personality type theory are provided as a guide for your self-assessment and understanding.

Everyone can carry out a wide range of work activities. You are likely to see aspects of yourself in more than one of the eight ways of working. However, research shows that each individual prefers one of these eight approaches. This core preference defines your characteristic approach to work. The other approaches support, and are secondary to, your preferred approach. As you develop skills and experience, you learn to use all of these approaches to facilitate your success. By understanding your first and most trusted approach, you can see how the other approaches flow and develop from it.

Moving in a career direction that uses your natural preferences increases your chances of career success. When you identify your work preferences, you can find strengths to build on. You also can figure out what parts of work may be more challenging for you. Throughout this book, personality type will help you customize your career success strategies.

Eight Ways of Working

Read the eight descriptions that follow. Identify which approach seems most natural and comfortable. Compare these descriptions with your four-letter type code to be sure you have identified your personal preferences accurately.

Responders: Act and Adapt Personality Types: ESTP and ESFP

Responders react immediately to the environment around them by acting. They are observant and quick to see problems and opportunities. They tend to be spontaneous and respond to things that are happening right now. They like to take practical actions that don't require a lot of pondering. Responders enjoy improvising, changing, and maneuvering. They may be good at fixing things and troubleshooting. They may enjoy handling emergencies or solving practical problems.

We all use this approach while observing and responding to our immediate environment. For example, as you hammer a nail, you note if the nail is bent and adjust the direction and strength of the next blow accordingly. But Responders go beyond this general tendency. They prefer and are drawn to activities that focus on direct observation and action. They are in tune with and focused on the world of actions and reactions.

If you are a Responder, you may not be highly motivated to complete self-assessments, especially if they require filling out paperwork and completing a long-term plan. Your career and life goals likely translate into practical, immediate actions to improve your situation. When setting goals, you should consider ways to add flexibility and variety to your lifestyle. Focus on what you enjoy doing now, and find ways to make your daily activities stimulating and interactive. Being engaged in the here and now, you may miss opportunities to position yourself effectively for the future. Challenge yourself to make longer-term as well as immediate goals.

Characteristic strengths of Responders

- Active
- Practical
- Adaptive
- Engaging
- Living in the moment

Work preferences of Responders

- Having fun and being playful
- Doing a variety of hands-on activities
- Being practical and using common sense
- Improvising and taking action
- Working on the most immediate task at hand
- Focusing on the here and now rather than the future

Explorers: Innovate and Initiate Personality Types: ENTP and ENFP

Explorers constantly look for associations and patterns. They like to link ideas and find connections; they prefer imagining what could be to focusing on what is. Explorers see possibilities in everything they sense, experience, and imagine. Explorers are enthusiastically and outwardly focused on the future, and like to initiate change. They see every situation as an opportunity to try something different, and they are drawn to work in which they must anticipate the future and create new ideas.

Everyone uses this approach at times; when imagining a new way of doing something, we look for potential. But Explorers prefer and are highly drawn to activities that provide opportunities to find and use patterns for creating new possibilities.

If you are an Explorer, you see themes and integrate information easily when you complete a self-assessment. You usually enjoy completing inventories and collecting and comparing information from a variety of sources. Your career and life goals likely include many options and possibilities for the future. When setting goals, you should consider ways to broaden your alternatives. Focus on setting broad, long-term goals that integrate your multiple interests. Because you are so engaged in ideas and possibilities, you may miss opportunities to position yourself effectively in the here and now. Challenge yourself to make short-term as well as long-term goals.

Characteristic strengths of Explorers

- Enthusiastic
- Inspired
- Open to change
- Multiple interests
- Flexible

Work preferences of Explorers

- Sharing and talking about ideas
- Seeking change and initiating new projects
- Creating new ways of doing things
- Improvising rather than preparing
- Multitasking
- Focusing on possibilities for the future

Expeditors: Direct and Decide Personality Types: ESTJ and ENTJ

Expeditors like to use logical analysis. They usually are quick to critique situations and spot flaws. They like to be organized and efficient, and they pride themselves on accomplishing as much as possible in the least amount of time. Expeditors like to solve problems, make decisions, complete tasks efficiently, and be in charge. They are likely to analyze a situation quickly, take control, and mobilize people to get the job done.

Everyone uses this logical, analytical approach at times, to detect flaws, list pros and cons, or organize tasks. But Expeditors prefer and are highly drawn to activities requiring analysis and active organization of people and resources to complete tasks.

If you are an Expeditor, you need a logical reason to complete a self-assessment, and you want to apply the information you learn immediately. When setting goals, you should consider exactly what you want to accomplish through work and why. Focus on finding logical and effective ways to achieve results. When you take a logical approach to goal setting, you may miss opportunities to incorporate others' needs and opinions. Challenge yourself to consider how working toward and achieving your career goals affects the people who are important to you.

Characteristic strengths of Expeditors

- Decisive
- Active
- Responsible
- Structured
- Results-oriented

Work preferences of Expeditors

- Analyzing and evaluating information
- Using a logical, decisive approach
- Working in a structured environment; being in control
- Organizing people and things
- Managing time and tasks
- Setting and achieving goals

Contributors: Communicate and Cooperate Personality Types: ESFJ and ENFJ

Contributors focus on personal relationships, values, opinions, and interactions. They strive to connect with others, create harmony, and cooperate. Contributors want to make sure everyone is happy and involved. They may be especially interested in organizing and coordinating events, processes, and activities to meet everyone's needs. Contributors naturally appreciate others and want to be appreciated for their uniqueness and efforts.

Everyone focuses on connecting with others when they remember a birthday, celebrate a success, engage in social or family traditions, or share a loss. But Contributors prefer and are highly drawn to activities that allow active communication and cooperation.

If you are a Contributor, you generally enjoy the process of self-assessment and are interested in discussions about self-improvement. Find ways to achieve your career and life goals through collaboration. When setting goals, you naturally consider and incorporate the needs of people close to you. Focus on who and what is important to you; consider how your career and life goals fit into a lifestyle that respects and accommodates significant others. Don't focus so much on others' needs that you minimize or ignore your own goals.

Characteristic strengths of Contributors

- Collaborative
- Cooperative
- Organized
- Harmonious
- Expressive

Work preferences of Contributors

- Coordinating people to achieve results
- Establishing and maintaining relationships
- Collaborating with others to complete projects
- Developing rapport and using empathy
- Making sure everyone is included and accepted
- Enjoying traditions and celebrating people's successes

Assimilators: Specialize and Stabilize Personality Types: ISTJ and ISFJ

Assimilators like to take in detailed information and then spend time integrating the information with past experiences and knowledge. Assimilators often have a comprehensive and thorough understanding of topics that interest them. Assimilators draw on a rich accumulation of facts and experiences to make decisions and take action. When they approach a situation or solve a problem, they often take time to reflect on past experiences, remembering and using strategies that worked well.

Everyone retains and classifies facts and experiences to some extent; for example, we do this when we share information about our favorite type of car, music, or vacation. But Assimilators use this approach as their primary way of understanding and dealing with the world as they collect and organize facts and experiences.

If you are an Assimilator, when you complete a self-assessment you likely focus on specific examples, situations, and facts to identify your strengths and areas of expertise. Your career and life goals usually reflect a continuation of activities and work you have done in the past. When setting goals, assess what work activities have held your interest and build on your successes. As an Assimilator, you may be uncomfortable about trying the unknown. Be open to finding out more about unfamiliar work options.

Characteristic strengths of Assimilators

- Detailed
- Methodical
- Practical
- Task-focused
- Building on experience

Work preferences of Assimilators

- Having structure, routine, and predictability in the workplace
- Planning carefully before starting a task
- Taking one thing at a time; working systematically and carefully
- Using accuracy and precision
- Mastering the facts and learning about a topic of interest in detail
- Having quiet time to reflect on information and experiences

Visionaries: Interpret and Implement Personality Types: INTJ and INFJ

Visionaries take time to think about and find meaning in data, ideas, and experiences. They create and revise rich mental models to help them understand and interpret experiences. Visionaries are future-oriented. They look at possibilities and make complex plans for changing systems or improving processes.

Everyone uses this approach when studying and comparing theoretical models or interpreting data and ideas. But Visionaries use this approach as their primary way of interpreting the world.

If you are a Visionary, you want a comprehensive self-assessment that finds themes and synthesizes data from multiple sources. Your career and life goals likely place importance on integrated, long-term results. When setting goals, consider creating a vision, or overarching picture, of what you want your life to look like. Focus on finding life themes and connecting all parts of your life into a whole. When you focus on your vision of the future, you may miss practical, here-and-now opportunities. Challenge yourself to make your vision and goals concrete by listing specific actions you can take right away.

Characteristic strengths of Visionaries

- Integration of information
- Broad perspective
- Focus on the future
- Organization
- Follow-through

Work preferences of Visionaries

- Reflecting on the meaning underlying facts and experiences
- Learning about new ideas, models, and theories
- Looking at information in many different ways
- Thinking about and implementing complex, long-term solutions
- Planning projects thoroughly before taking action
- Using metaphors, symbols, and other abstract figures of speech

Analyzers: Examine and Evaluate Personality Types: ISTP and INTP

Analyzers take time to analyze information and make logical decisions. When presented with a problem or task, they collect data, ask themselves questions, and consider the best course of action. Analyzers relate principles of science, technology, or other areas of expertise to problem solving and find ways to test their conclusions. An Analyzer enjoys trying things to see what happens.

Everyone uses this approach when thinking about problems or making logical decisions. But Analyzers use this approach as their primary way of interpreting the world.

If you are an Analyzer, you may be skeptical about assessment tools. You rely on your own judgment rather than others' opinions or assessment results. Be aware that you can miss out on important information by dismissing feedback that doesn't fit with your own judgment. When setting goals, consider your options and choose logical goals to improve your situation. Focus on what you want from your career and why. Because you tend to focus on objective analysis, you may not consider others' needs. As you set your goals, challenge yourself to seek input from people close to you.

Characteristic strengths of Analyzers

- Adaptable
- Flexible
- Analytical
- Self-reliant
- Independent

Work preferences of Analyzers

- Internally questioning and analyzing why and how things are done
- Finding out why and how things work
- Solving problems and improvising
- Seeking logical connections to new information
- Using objectivity and approaching situations in a logical manner
- Working independently in a changing, challenging environment

Enhancers: Care and Connect Personality Types: ISFP and INFP

Enhancers create personal relationships to situations. They are thoughtful and tend to focus on how situations and circumstances affect others. Enhancers are careful to accommodate people and make others' needs a priority. They assess and evaluate situations by relating them to personal and human values.

Everyone uses this approach in some aspects of their lives: for example, when choosing what pictures to put into a scrapbook for a friend, or deciding how to customize a recipe to suit the tastes of a specific group. But Enhancers seek to understand and relate experience to values as their primary way of interpreting the world.

If you are an Enhancer, you are interested in self-assessment, especially as a way of determining what is personally meaningful. Because you focus on others, you may minimize your contributions and need encouragement to highlight your own abilities and accomplishments. When setting goals, consider your core values. Determine what is most important to you. Focus on expressing yourself authentically through your work and your goals. But as you focus on finding work that is personally meaningful, try to logically analyze your goals to make sure they are attainable.

Characteristic strengths of Enhancers

- Authentic
- Appreciative
- Nurturing
- Flexible
- Harmonious

Work preferences of Enhancers

- Quietly expressing one's self and values through work
- Appreciating and working to improve the world
- Staying in the background to support others
- Working in harmonious, collaborative, and supportive environments
- Controlling work pace and structure
- Having flexibility, variety, and time for reflection

Which of these eight natural ways of working sounds most like your own? Does your way of working align with your four-letter code? If not, you may want to review the four pairs of personality preferences. If your natural way of working is not clear, clarify your preferences by doing additional reading on personality type or by contacting a professional trained in interpreting the MBTI® tool.

My natural way of working is: _____

What Does Career Success Look Like for You?

Career success means something different to everyone. Only you, and perhaps those closest to you, can understand fully what *your* successful career looks like. To achieve career success, you must know how you prefer to work and what you prefer to do. This knowledge is based on your work interests, skills, values, constraints, and preferences, though you need to know what lifestyle you desire as well. When you know yourself, you can apply this personal knowledge to your career and life goals. Career and life goals can guide your decision making and help you choose a course of action. When you know your career and life goals, you can more easily recognize and capitalize on opportunities to ensure career success. Here are some questions to help you think about what career success means to you.

Skills, interests, and personality preferences

- What are you good at?
- What do you enjoy doing?
- What is really hard for you to do?
- What do you dislike doing?
- What skills do you enjoy using and developing?
- Do you want to learn something new? What would you like to learn?
- What activities do you enjoy that can generate income?

Values and lifestyle

- What do you value?
- When, where, and how much do you want to work?
- Where do you want to live?
- What do you want to do in the time you spend outside work?
- Do you have physical or psychological limitations? How do these limitations affect your choices?
- Do you want to make lifestyle changes? What changes?

Financial needs and wants

- How much money do you need to make?
- How much money do you want to make?
- If you change your lifestyle, how will this affect the amount of money you need or want?

Life roles

- What life roles are important to you (e.g., parent, spouse, friend, community member)?
- What time commitments do you want to make to these roles?
- What are the needs of the significant people in your life who influence your career?

Set Career Goals

When you have answered these questions, you can create goals for yourself. As you set your career goals, consider what types of work suit your work style, interests, values, lifestyle, and constraints. Review your natural way of working to define what you want to get out of your career and to help you refine your goals.

Setting goals helps you define what you want to do and where you want to be. Carefully consider what you want your career to do for you. This positions you for career and life success.

You may have specific financial goals, based on your past experience in the workforce. When setting career goals based on finances, think about your lifestyle preferences. Separate your financial *needs* from your financial *wants*. We live in a materialistic society, where many of us feel considerable pressure to buy lots of "stuff"—cars, vacation homes, and other consumer goods. All this buying often results in financial stress and debt. Think about whether you want your "wants" to determine your lifestyle. Decide for yourself if "keeping up with the Joneses" is really an important life or career goal for you. You can be very comfortable surviving on less income if you focus on your needs rather than your wants. And when you control your finances, you broaden your career choices.

Money is not the only consideration when you set your career goals. Many people leave high-paying work and long work hours to move into lower-paying or part-time work; their goal is to reduce stress, spend more time with family, or pursue nonwork pastimes. Other people set career goals based on nonmonetary factors; they may care more about expressing themselves artistically or making a contribution to society. Still others seek opportunities to connect and share ideas through their work. Learning, developing expertise, achieving results, gaining flexibility, or achieving stability may be other themes important to you when defining your career goals.

Family needs can be a major influence on your career goals. For example, the birth of a child, divorce from a spouse who was filling a childcare role, or the needs of aging parents may become important considerations. Explore whether personal situations such as these affect your life or work goals, either directly or indirectly.

In addition to family commitments, you may have community, religious, or humanitarian goals that influence your work choices. These goals may be clear and simple, such as not wanting to work on a certain day of the week, or they may be more complex, such as wanting to do work that has a positive effect on the environment.

Keep in mind that work doesn't necessarily mean a full-time, 9-to-5 commitment. You have plenty of options. You can have one or more part-time jobs, start a business, do contract or project work, take seasonal work, work only evenings and weekends, share a job, or make a profit from a hobby. You may be able to create work if you see a need and approach an employer. Consider these various ways of generating income as you refine your career goals.

Tips for setting career and life goals

- Remember, these are *your* career and life goals. Base them on your own work and lifestyle needs and preferences. Take a careful inventory of what is important to you and those close to you.
- Define what success looks like for you; avoid the temptation to define your success in terms of what others or society might view as successful.
- Make your goals specific and concrete. Translate them into realistic statements of what you want next. There is nothing wrong with having big dreams for the future, as long as you take practical steps toward them.
- If you have multiple goals, prioritize them.
- Be aware of potential conflicts in your goals. For example, if the kind of work you want to do is not compatible with where you want to live, you will not be able to achieve both these goals at the same time.
- Post or write your goals where you can review them.
- Make a plan to work toward your goals. Set tasks to accomplish, with timelines. Measure and reward your progress. Allow some flexibility in your plan to deal with unexpected changes, surprises, and opportunities.
- Persist in pursuing your goals, but be open to changing them if your priorities and situation shift. In these cases, don't give up on your goals, but redefine them.

Reflection and Action

This chapter shows why asking yourself for directions is essential. Those striving for career success understand who they are and set individualized career goals. Now that you have identified your personality type and your characteristic strengths and work preferences, you can use this information to ensure you are heading in a career direction that works for you. In the area below, summarize what you have learned about your personality type. Highlight your characteristic strengths and work preferences from the chapter. Then describe your career and life goals to make sure you are headed in a career direction that suits who you are.

CHAPTER THREE

Optimize Your Outlook

When you optimize your outlook, you strive to be as helpful and upbeat as possible in everyday interactions. You deal with problems confidently. When faced with challenges, you see possibilities and opportunities. You see the best in people and situations. Other people, in turn, see you as energetic, alert, and positive. They like being around you because you are pleasant and hopeful. They see that you enjoy your work, and they are inspired by your enthusiasm and zest for life.

Optimizing your attitude can enhance your chances of career success greatly. Employers, potential customers, or clients quickly assess your words, body language, and behaviors to decide if you are someone they want to talk to, hire, work with, or promote. Employers are constantly looking for people with the "right attitude" or a "positive outlook."

People don't want to interact with someone who is negative and complains constantly. Negative people drain energy from others and are not any fun to be around. They make people uncomfortable and situations unpleasant. People with a negative or pessimistic attitude create a bad impression of both themselves and their workplace.

Most work involves some form of service to others. In a service environment, the customer's experience is of utmost importance. If employees have a negative outlook, customers are likely to have a bad experience. They may choose not to return to a place of business where they were served by a person with a negative outlook. Clearly, negativity is not the path to career success.

What Is Your Outlook?

You may not be aware of the outlook you are sharing with the world, but others see it right away. Your outlook may reflect ways of responding to situations that, over time, have become unconscious and automatic. These habits—including the way you dress, walk, stand, and talk—show your attitude and greatly influence your career success.

People's outlooks fall on a continuum between highly optimistic and very pessimistic. Optimists tend to expect and hope for the best, whereas pessimists expect the worst.

Success Story: About Face

Here is an example of someone who was not aware of her outlook and how it affected others and her career. This woman's personality type preferences were ESTP. At work meetings, she became frustrated when her points were not well received by the group; she slouched and frowned and stopped contributing. When her supervisor discussed these behaviors, the woman admitted she tended to shut down when she was frustrated. She knew she needed to make an effort to stay engaged. She had no idea her facial expressions bothered people, however. Her supervisor suggested that she look into a mirror while reimagining a frustrating situation. The woman was shocked to see how overtly her emotion was reflected in her expression. After that, she worked on controlling the way she came across to others.

Your outlook affects others, but it greatly affects *you* as well. It influences how you see yourself and how you interpret and react to situations. Positive beliefs about yourself and your ability to meet challenges and accomplish goals are valuable assets. You need to dream and have lofty goals and visions—that's what allows you to attempt and accomplish things others might believe are impossible. Optimistic thinking can provide the drive and initiative you need.

There is a phenomenon in psychology known as the self-fulfilling prophecy: If you believe you can accomplish something, you will. If you think you can't do something, you likely won't be able to. Consider what that means for you. If you are constantly focusing on negative outcomes to situations, perhaps you are contributing to those negative outcomes.

Of course, you need to do more than simply *think* you can accomplish something. Not everything you believe will come to be just because of your beliefs. Thinking optimistically about what will happen is only a starting point. You still need to put effort into achieving your goals. And optimistic thinking won't protect you from all of life's challenges and setbacks. However, when you believe in yourself and in positive outcomes, you are more likely to achieve your desires. In addition, others will be attracted to your positive outlook; they'll want to be around you and help you.

The following checklists help you see what kind of attitude you are showing to the world. The first checklist describes a pessimistic approach; the second describes an optimistic approach. Check off your typical behaviors. Then strive to minimize any of the behaviors you checked in the first list and maximize behaviors in the second list.

Signs of a pessimistic attitude

- ☐ Frowning and slouching
- ☐ Ignoring, avoiding, or showing little interest in others
- ☐ Putting others down or passing on negative gossip
- ☐ Putting yourself down
- ☐ Predicting negative outcomes to situations
- ☐ Complaining or expressing anger and frustration

Signs of an optimistic attitude

- ☐ Greeting and acknowledging others in a friendly manner
- ☐ Saying mostly positive things about others and situations
- ☐ Predicting realistic, positive outcomes
- ☐ Dealing gracefully with unpleasant realities
- ☐ Seeing opportunities and solutions in problematic situations
- ☐ Having realistic expectations for yourself and others

What Is Affecting Your Outlook?

If you have a negative outlook and make a less than optimal impression on others, you need to find out why. This requires some soul searching. When you address the factors that contribute to your outlook, you can start to become more positive.

Factors that can affect your outlook include your personal situation, work environment, stress level, self-confidence, health, commitment to work, and expectations. The following section discusses each of these factors and provides tips for optimizing your outlook. Remember, a negative outlook may have become habitual for you, so be patient. It takes time to replace old habits with new behaviors.

Success Story: Do You Want Fries with That?

This example demonstrates how an individual can learn to project a positive outlook. A young man with ISTJ personality type preferences started work in a customer service role. He was, by nature, quietly competent but not outwardly enthusiastic, so customer service wasn't a natural fit for him. He realized that to succeed in his job, he needed to make a plan for greeting and serving customers. He developed a routine that included smiling, greeting, taking the order in a pleasant voice, nodding his head, maintaining eye contact, and thanking the customer at the end of the transaction. He put effort into expressing his positive attitude to others, and his effort paid off.

Manage difficult personal situations

Your personal situation can strongly influence your outlook. Almost everyone has been dispirited or pessimistic at times. Everyone sometimes feels tired, stressed, unmotivated, or overwhelmed by events and situations in their life. At these times it is difficult to be optimistic or show a positive attitude.

If your outlook has changed dramatically and quickly, it may be because of a significant event in your personal life such as a divorce, the death of someone close to you, health problems, financial problems, or conflicts with others. It is very difficult to be optimistic when you are going through intense personal or interpersonal difficulties. Sometimes such events can lead to intense sadness, anger, fear, or frustration.

In these situations, a caring friend or family member may help you sort out your emotions and give you ideas and support to get you back on track. But avoid conversations in which you only wallow and complain. Getting stuck in a "poor me" mindset won't solve anything. Consider seeking assistance from a trained professional, such as a psychologist or counselor, who can help you manage your situation. If situational factors make it difficult to do your work, look into taking a leave from the workplace or adjusting your work hours.

Manage difficult work situations

Sometimes work situations make it difficult to maintain an optimal outlook. Employees often get in the habit of complaining about their workplace and its leaders, decisions, and processes. This may lead to or build on negativity.

Many aspects of the workplace can be stressful. Some people find routine stressful; others are bothered by unpredictability. Incompetence, disorder, poor morale, and interpersonal conflicts cause dissatisfaction, as do inadequate pay, lack of recognition, and unappealing hours and tasks. Also, negativity can increase when no one seems to listen to or act on employee concerns.

> ### *Excel Your Way:*
> ### *Tips for Thinking (T) and Feeling (F) Types*
>
> If you are a Thinking (T) type, you may have an especially hard time working with incompetent people or in disorderly environments. If you are a Feeling (F) type, interpersonal conflict and morale issues make it very difficult for you to be positive at work.

Work stress increases in times of change and uncertainty. During such periods, people worry about job loss or increased workloads. Employees who lack information about change tend to fill the gap with rumors and speculation, creating fear. You can't avoid uncertainty; all you can do is try your best to anticipate change and adapt to it. Strategies to help you manage change and uncertainty are included in Chapter 10. If your work is undergoing lots of change and you find this very stressful, you may need to consider alternative work options.

If you are very unhappy in your work, you may be working in the wrong place or doing the wrong tasks. Take a fresh look at your work and ask yourself if what you do is meeting your needs and preferences. Note the tasks you enjoy and the ones you dislike.

Look for ways to change your duties. Perhaps you can move into a different role or exchange tasks with a coworker. If most of your day is filled with unsatisfying tasks, maybe you need to consider finding a different kind of work.

Sometimes it is the atmosphere, morale, or values of the people or organization you work with that add to your dissatisfaction with work. Think about how you are treated by others at work and evaluate if you like the way your employer treats the people who work for the company. Note the number of conflicts and frustrations involved in your day-to-day interactions. You may be able to bring attention to and resolve some interpersonal issues, but, if you work in a highly toxic environment, sometimes the best option is getting out.

No matter what the source of your frustration and dissatisfaction at work, you really have only three options: ignore the negative aspects, resolve the problems, or move out of the situation. Ignoring small irritants may be a solution if you are generally happy in your work. However, ignoring larger problems can lead to long-term stress and frustration. At some point you will need to decide to take action by either dealing with the source of your dissatisfaction, or if that is not possible, modifying or changing your work environment.

Success Story: Get Me Out of Here

Some personality types may be especially sensitive to working in an unsupportive environment. A woman with ENFJ personality type preferences entered career counseling because she hated going to work. She had become highly critical and frustrated in her job. After completing a self-assessment, she realized she enjoyed the work she was doing, but she disliked the way the people in her workplace treated each other. As a result of her career counseling, she ended up at another company doing almost exactly the same work. The difference was the people. In her new organization, people worked collaboratively and encouraged each other. In this environment, she was more successful and had greater work satisfaction.

What is the atmosphere and morale in your work environment? Do you enjoy your work, or do you find yourself complaining about it frequently? If you're unhappy, you may need to decide what you can and can't change about your work situation. You want to deal with work issues you can resolve and avoid falling into the habit of complaining.

Complaining to coworkers rarely changes anything and may make your days at work even more unpleasant. If you want to voice your concerns, consider whom you need to talk to and how to approach them. Chapter 6, Relate to Anyone, shows you how to best approach these communications.

> ## Excel Your Way:
> ## Tips for Extraverts (E) and Introverts (I)
>
> If you have a preference for Extraversion (E), you may express your complaints and negative emotions quite vocally. Think before you speak, especially if your comments might damage customer relations or organizational morale. As well, be careful about expressing negative body language.
>
> If you have a preference for Introversion (I), you may be less likely to share your feelings and thoughts at work. Try showing more outward enthusiasm and expressing your positive attitude with body language.

Minimize stress

Everyone experiences stress. At reasonable levels, stress can stimulate you to perform well. At unreasonable levels, it does the opposite.

When you are under stress, your body releases adrenaline. Adrenaline causes your blood pressure to rise, pumps sugar into your blood, and prepares your body to act. This response is healthy in situations where you need to confront or run away from danger. However, staying in this high-alert mode for extended periods can have many negative effects on your mental and physical health.

Among other things, stress affects sleep. When people are in stressful situations, they tend to lose sleep, which diminishes energy and alertness. It is hard to be upbeat and optimistic when you are exhausted.

Stress affects everyone differently. What is stressful for one person may not be stressful for someone else. Similarly, a strategy for managing stress may be helpful for one person but not for another. The key is to understand how you react to your environment. Learning to recognize when your stress level rises, and why, are the first steps in managing stress.

Excel Your Way: Tips for Extraverts (E) and Introverts (I)

If you have a preference for Extraversion (E), you may find yourself exaggerating your outward behaviors when you experience stress. Look for these cues that you are under stress: You may find yourself talking more than usual, becoming more impatient, and taking action with less thought than usual.

If you have a preference for Introversion (I), you may find yourself turning inward when you experience stress. Look for these cues that you are under stress: You may find yourself withdrawing, being less talkative than normal, or taking longer to make decisions.

To understand your stress reaction, monitor your stress levels. This will help you see when your stress becomes uncomfortable. Note what is happening when you start experiencing an uncomfortable amount of stress. Your stress may be triggered by events, thoughts, feelings, or interactions. When you are under too much stress, you may experience symptoms such as anxiety, fear, anger, and impatience. You may note changes in the way you think about situations; you may not be as optimistic, hopeful, or confident. You may also experience physical symptoms such as headaches, stomachaches, tense muscles, or changes in sleep patterns.

Personality type can help you understand what activities may be stressful for you. Each personality type naturally prefers different work activities and ways of interacting. For example, one person may be very comfortable working in an environment that emphasizes structure, predictability, and routine; another person may find this kind of environment very stressful. At the end of this chapter, you will find common stressors and stress reactions for different personality types. Use these to identify signs that you are becoming stressed and to help you understand what triggers your stress.

Excel Your Way: Tips for Judging (J) and Perceiving (P) types

If you have a preference for Judging (J), you are most comfortable when situations are structured and somewhat predictable. You may experience stress when unexpected events interrupt your schedule. Build some flexibility into your planning to minimize the effects of disruptions.

If you have a preference for Perceiving (P), completing tasks under time pressure usually energizes you. However, at times you may feel stressed when deadlines are too tight. Be sure to schedule sufficient time so you can complete your tasks without undue stress.

When you monitor your stress, you can take action to minimize it before it becomes unmanageable. Look at the list of stress-management strategies below, and figure out which ones may work for you. Generally speaking, you want to engage in activities or thoughts that are calming or that eliminate or reduce sources of stress. Later in the chapter you will find additional strategies for changing your outlook and managing your stress.

Strategies for managing stress

- When possible, deal directly with your stressors. For example, if you experience stress when you have a conflict with someone, figure out how to resolve the conflict. If your work is highly stressful, you may need to find new work.
- Connect with others for support and encouragement.
- Balance work and play. Determine how you want to spend your time. Don't neglect your hobbies and interests.
- Balancing multiple roles and responsibilities may be stressful. Take inventory of all your roles and responsibilities. Find ways to minimize, eliminate, negotiate, or simplify some of those roles.
- Take care of yourself. Eat well. Exercise. Sleep. Indulge in comforting self-care rituals such as a hot bath or a massage.
- Learn new things to increase your work and leisure options.

- Avoid having unrealistic expectations for yourself or others. Don't expect everything to be perfect. Allow yourself to be human. You will make mistakes; so will everyone else.
- Engage in spiritual or religious activities. Many people find it comforting to connect to some form of higher power or belief system.

Build your confidence

Lack of self-confidence may also affect your outlook. People who lack confidence in their abilities or don't think they are as good as others may become defensive or pessimistic. Those with low confidence may act unsure of themselves and may seek constant approval. Alternatively, they may mask their lack of self-confidence with a cocky demeanor.

You can boost your confidence in a number of ways. The following list provides some general techniques to increase your confidence. But remember: It takes time and effort to become more confident, so don't expect big changes in a short time.

Confidence builders

- Identify and focus on your strengths
- Surround yourself with supportive people
- Set and meet small, realistic goals
- Acknowledge and celebrate your successes
- Keep your expectations realistic
- Be grateful for what you have rather than focusing on what you don't have
- Avoid comparisons; don't judge yourself by others' standards
- Keep your thoughts positive
- Walk, talk, and dress confidently

What you say to yourself—your self-talk—has a powerful effect on your confidence. To build your confidence, you may need to change your self-talk. To assess and change your self-talk, pay careful attention to what you say to others about yourself. Also monitor what you think about yourself and your capabilities. Create a list of negative or limiting statements you hear yourself saying or thinking. (Don't neglect the thinking part; much self-talk is internal.) Here are some common examples.

Self-limiting talk

- I can't do this.
- This is really hard for me.
- I'm not good at . . .
- I'll never be any good at . . .

To optimize your outlook, reframe, or change, your limiting statements into more positive ones. Be sure the new messages you are telling yourself are realistic and believable. If you think you are inept at managing time, don't tell yourself you are wonderful at managing time. Try a more realistic replacement such as "I can focus on managing my time more effectively by using my planner."

Using positive self-talk isn't the same as ignoring or minimizing areas of difficulty. Everyone has flaws. Your challenge is to accept yourself as a human who is striving to learn and grow. Of course, some things are difficult for you. That's O.K. Your goal is not perfection or mastery of everything. Rather, your goal is to see yourself, and your efforts, in a positive way. Realistic and hopeful self-talk statements help you build your confidence.

Realistic self-affirmations

- I am basically a good person.
- I try to do my best.
- I have strengths and challenges.
- I am as good and worthwhile as anyone else.
- I am not perfect, but I keep developing and learning.
- Everyone struggles sometimes. I've just got to keep on trying.
- Everyone makes mistakes. I can learn from my mistakes.

Take care of yourself

You require energy and alertness to tackle daily tasks and maintain an optimal outlook. When you are rested and alert, you can focus effectively; when you are tired or distracted, you may make mistakes and engage in unsafe work practices. The company you work for is entitled to expect top performance from its workforce. This is also true if you work for yourself. You are responsible for attending work regularly, maintaining your energy and alertness, and attending to any conditions that may endanger you or others in the workplace.

Make an effort to live a healthy lifestyle and maintain a balance between work, other responsibilities, and recreational time. Getting enough sleep, eating well, and exercising will boost your energy level and make it easier for you to see situations in a more positive way. You already know that a healthy lifestyle helps you manage stress. These behaviors also boost your immune system so you are less likely to get sick.

If you suspect you have a physical or mental health problem, visit a physician. He or she can help you learn about and manage health issues.

Excel Your Way: Tips for Sensing (S) and Intuitive (N) Types

If you have a preference for Sensing (S), you are likely tuned in to the practical realities of situations. Turn your sensing inward to assess your physical state. Use your awareness to maximize your energy and health.

If you have a preference for Intuition (N), you may not be well attuned to your physical cues. You may sometimes ignore messages from your body about basic states such as energy level and hunger. Learn to pay attention to what your body is telling you.

Show commitment to your work

Your everyday behaviors signal your outlook. Look at your behaviors through the eyes of your customers or employer. Some behaviors indicate you are simply putting in time and are not committed to your work. Look through the following list to assess whether you show up ready and willing to work every day. These basic behaviors set the stage for a positive commitment and outlook.

Demonstrating your commitment

- Get to work a few minutes early so you are ready, and on the job, at or before your starting time.

- Arrive on time to meetings. Be prepared to discuss topics or issues.
- Take breaks when there is a natural slow-down in your work. Return from breaks promptly.
- Focus on the tasks at hand and strive to be productive.
- At the end of the day, finish the task at hand rather than just dropping it and leaving.
- Wear neat, clean, and appropriate clothing.
- Speak positively and use positive body language.
- When work is slow, look for additional work tasks to accomplish.
- Refrain from complaining about your employer.

Be realistic

You can take optimism too far. Being positive and hopeful is a powerful way to approach the world. However, if you avoid thinking about the possible negative results of situations or fail to consider the practical realities of situations, you are apt to do yourself a disservice. You may expect to complete tasks sooner than is humanly possible, and you may fail to anticipate problems. You may ignore or dismiss important issues, and others may feel that you gloss over their concerns.

It is important to think about what might go wrong and what might not work. When you predict and highlight potential roadblocks and challenges, you can use optimism to see past the problems, overcome barriers, and achieve the results you want.

The following list shows ways in which a positive approach can go overboard. Completing the checklist can help you assess if you are someone who tends to ignore rather than address life's challenges. If so, strive to keep positive without dismissing unpleasant realities.

Signs of an overly idealistic attitude

- ☐ Ignoring or avoiding unpleasant realities
- ☐ Being overly enthusiastic, even in situations where enthusiasm is inappropriate
- ☐ Focusing on ideals without considering facts, details, and status quo
- ☐ Setting unrealistic expectations for yourself and others
- ☐ Glossing over rather than dealing with barriers and constraints
- ☐ Minimizing others' problems or issues

Excel Your Way:
Tips for Thinking (T) and Feeling (F) Types

If you have a preference for Thinking (T), you tend to analyze and evaluate situations. In the workplace, you may tend to make skeptical or critical comments. You may need to curb this tendency in certain situations; others may interpret your critiques as pessimism.

Feeling (F) types, especially those who also have a preference for Extraversion (E), naturally show lots of enthusiasm and optimism. You may need to curb this tendency in some situations so others don't see you as overly idealistic or unrealistic.

Optimizing Your Outlook: Personality Type Strengths and Challenges

All personality types can optimize their outlook. Every personality type has unique strengths and challenges aligned to their natural preferences. Read through the information on your personality type for suggestions specifically tailored to your natural way of working.

Responders (ESTP and ESFP)

As a Responder, you generally come across as optimistic, active, and energetic. You naturally accept people and circumstances and don't worry much about situations beyond your control. Highly structured and routine work environments, especially ones where you have few opportunities to maneuver or adapt, may be stressful for you. You may also find it stressful to work on ambiguous tasks or to engage in activities that are highly conceptual and future-oriented rather than practical.

As a Responder, your first sign of stress may be an inability to focus. Your natural knack for responding quickly becomes exaggerated; your attention shifts quickly—too quickly—from one thing to the next. This is your cue to take action to minimize your stress. If your stress level becomes very high you may become immobilized and withdraw, worrying about all of the things that could possibly go wrong. If this occurs, redefine your priorities and make a new plan of action. Regain control by analyzing your situation and recognizing how unrealistic your worries are. You may need to enlist the help of others to accomplish these tasks.

Explorers (ENTP and ENFP)

As an Explorer, you usually are optimistic, enthusiastic, and idealistic. Others may be skeptical of your natural zeal, and you may need to tone down how you express yourself to gain credibility. Highly detailed work and heavily rule-bound environments that inhibit your flexibly and creativity may be especially stressful for you. You may also experience stress when you can't engage in open-ended exploration of ideas or when others are not enthusiastic about ideas and possibilities.

When you experience stress, you usually feel overwhelmed. Your natural strength for seeing new ideas and options becomes exaggerated; instead of feeling motivated by so many possibilities, you get lost in and weighed down by them. This is your cue to take action to minimize your stress. If your stress level increases, you may begin to withdraw from others or obsess about minor details. At this point, you may find it helpful to focus on self-care behaviors such as relaxation, exercise, and healthy eating. You may also want to review your commitments and eliminate or delegate responsibilities.

Expeditors (ESTJ and ENTJ)

As an Expeditor, you tend to critique and spot flaws, and you may not see the value of emphasizing positive aspects of situations. Challenge yourself to add more positive comments to your repertoire. You are likely to experience stress in disorganized and inefficient work environments. Incompetent coworkers and a lack of control cause stress as well.

Expeditors tend to react to stress by taking an overly critical and unyielding approach to situations. Your ability to act decisively and effectively becomes exaggerated; you begin to make decisions more quickly, with less consideration of the relevant data.

If your stress level becomes very high, you may withdraw and become highly emotional. At this point, you may find it helpful to share your feelings with someone you trust. Identifying what is important to you and deciding to focus on only these important tasks can also help you reduce your stress.

Contributors (ESFJ and ENFJ)

As a Contributor, you are generally highly positive and supportive. However, if your morale or organizational morale is low, you may act as an organizational barometer, measuring and focusing on everyone's concerns. When you are dissatisfied, you may find it difficult to present a positive outlook until everyone else's needs have been attended to. You are likely to experience stress in work environments characterized by conflict, confrontation, or criticism. Working with aloof or uncooperative coworkers, customers, or managers may also be stressful.

When you feel stressed, you may take on an excessive role in addressing interpersonal conflicts. You may get involved in situations you'd be better off avoiding; you may try to help those who aren't interested in working out their problems. Your ability to support and connect others becomes exaggerated as you begin to push too hard for interpersonal harmony, rather than facilitate it. If your stress level continues to rise, you may become overly critical and evaluate situations harshly. At this point, consider taking some time alone for self-care, and focus on what is important. Talking to someone who is not involved in your work situation also can be helpful.

Assimilators (ISTJ and ISFJ)

As an Assimilator, you usually don't show high levels of enthusiasm unless you are discussing familiar and well-researched topics or talking to people you know and trust. You are likely to experience stress in rapidly changing or unstructured work settings or in environments in which your roles are ambiguous. Insufficient or inaccurate information and inefficient work processes also contribute to your stress.

Your first sign of stress is usually an excessive attention to detail. Your natural thoroughness becomes exaggerated as you grow preoccupied by small and even irrelevant details. If your stress level becomes very high, you may act impulsively or imagine all sorts of negative possibilities. If this occurs, you may find it helpful to take some time alone and begin to focus on achieving small, realistic goals. You may also reduce your stress and boost your confidence by recalling previous situations in which you demonstrated your competence or expertise.

Visionaries (INTJ and INFJ)

As a Visionary, you typically have an optimistic, forward-thinking, and idealistic outlook. You may need to translate your views into practical terms so others will understand your outlook and won't see you as unrealistic or impractical. You are likely to experience stress in noisy or distracting work environments or environments in which you have to complete routine tasks, deal with many details, or violate your principles. Working for or with poorly performing managers or coworkers is also stressful for Visionaries.

When you start to experience stress, you exaggerate your natural ability to interpret and integrate information, attempting to link a plethora of ideas without verifiable connections. If your stress level becomes very high, you may begin to fixate on small details or lose yourself in food, exercise, television, games, or other activities in the external, sensory world. At this point, you may find it helpful to retreat and take quiet time alone to refocus and revitalize. Avoid dealing with details and highly structured routines, at least until you are recharged.

Analyzers (ISTP and INTP)

As an Analyzer, you tend to be doubtful, skeptical, and analytical rather than optimistic. Because you don't see optimism as necessary or appealing, you need to find logical reasons for presenting a favorable outlook. You may feel stress in work environments that are highly interactive, inefficient, rule-bound, or inequitable. You find it especially stressful to work with incompetent people, especially if your work is linked to or dependent on theirs.

The first sign of stress for an Analyzer is usually an increase in negativity and cynicism. Your objectivity and logical evaluation become exaggerated, and you disregard alternative perspectives. As your stress level grows, your objective criticism may turn personal, and you may become overly sensitive to criticism from others. At this point, you may find it helpful to disengage from the situation to regain your composure. When possible, step back from tasks and interactions. Look for new information to help you view the situation from an alternative, more positive perspective.

Enhancers (ISFP and INFP)

As an Enhancer, you tend to be quietly positive and optimistic. But when you are in a situation that creates an internal conflict with your personal values, you may show a negative and critical outlook to the world. You are likely to experience stress in highly interactive, structured work environments with immediate and multiple demands. A work situation that involves conflict and confrontation, or work that violates your core values, also can be a great source of stress.

Your first sign of stress is usually an enhanced sensitivity and a rigid adherence to your point of view. Your natural unassuming, personal approach becomes exaggerated as you react negatively to perceived criticism from others. As your stress level increases, you may begin to doubt your competence and become critical and judgmental toward others. If this occurs, you may find it helpful to take time alone to refocus on your personal strengths and values. Enjoyable interactions with significant others can help you regain your connections.

Reflection and Action

This chapter shows why optimizing your outlook is essential. Optimistic individuals show a positive outlook and confidently deal with difficult situations. They minimize and manage stress and take care of themselves. How can you optimize your outlook? Is anything standing in your way? What environments and activities are difficult or stressful for you? Look at your responses to the checklists in this chapter and think about the suggestions offered. In the area below, write out some steps you can take to optimize your outlook.

CHAPTER FOUR

Put Yourself in Charge

When you put yourself in charge of your career, you give yourself the authority to make choices and take action to be successful. Putting yourself in charge means you take ownership for your mistakes and achievements. You stand behind and are accountable for what you say and do. When you are in charge, you work independently, persist, and follow through on tasks. People know they can count on you. They see you as committed, determined, dependable, reliable, and dedicated—all qualities much needed and rewarded in the workforce.

When you take ownership of your actions, you acknowledge your role in events and situations. You critique your actions to discover what worked well and what you need to change. When you acknowledge that your actions did not produce the result you were hoping for, you adjust and improve. You also acknowledge, celebrate, and build on your strengths and accomplishments. When you take personal responsibility, you learn and improve.

People who don't take ownership of their actions appear unmotivated, passive, complaining, dependent, or helpless. When things go wrong, they blame others and ignore or deny their role. In today's society, it's all too common to blame others or circumstances when things go wrong rather than taking responsibility for our actions and results. People often spend more time and energy trying to absolve themselves of responsibility than they do acknowledging ownership and correcting or compensating for errors and flaws.

If you put blame elsewhere when you don't achieve expected results, you are unlikely to improve your performance. You become immersed in blaming, passing off responsibility, and making excuses. When you take this approach, you see failures and even successes as events beyond your control—attributable to luck, chance, or others' actions. You become a victim of circumstances.

When you think this way, you decrease your productivity. Instead of dealing with mistakes and problems, you cover them up. No one wants to hire, recommend, or promote someone who does not take responsibility for his or her actions. You will find it virtually impossible to create your ideal career if you believe factors outside your efforts are responsible for your success or failure. If you want a successful career, you need to take charge of your actions and progress. By taking responsibility for your actions, working independently, and persisting on tasks, you put yourself in charge and greatly increase your chances of career success.

Do You Take Ownership of Your Actions?

What you say and do provides clues about whether you are putting yourself in charge. Read through the following lists and check off statements that describe your typical response to situations. Strive to minimize the use of behaviors in the first list and maximize the use of behaviors in the second list.

Evidence that you are not taking ownership of your actions

- ☐ Blaming others for problems and situations
- ☐ Blaming others for lack of results
- ☐ Making excuses for lack of results
- ☐ Asserting your inability to do something
- ☐ Not attempting tasks
- ☐ Denying, ignoring, or detaching from your faults

☐ Trusting luck or fate for success or failure
☐ Requiring a lot of day-to-day assistance or supervision
☐ Easily giving up

Evidence that you are taking ownership of your actions

☐ Acknowledging your contribution to problems and situations
☐ Taking responsibility when desired results are not achieved
☐ Making no excuses for lack of results
☐ Expressing belief in your ability to accomplish goals
☐ Attempting tasks, even when you are unsure of the outcome
☐ Admitting to your faults
☐ Linking your efforts to your successes
☐ Working independently on day-to-day tasks
☐ Persisting on tasks

Take more ownership

To take more ownership of your actions, start by looking at your current habits. Keep a mental tally of how you respond to others. Note what you say and do. Phrases such as "It doesn't matter what I do" or "It's not my fault" or "There is nothing I can do" reveal a sense of powerlessness or a detachment from personal ownership.

When you hear yourself saying or thinking such things, reframe your thoughts to focus on more useful ways of interpreting the situation, such as "What can I do differently?" or "How did I contribute to this situation?" or "How can I fix this?" Owning your actions means you acknowledge your imperfections. You give yourself permission to try new things, make mistakes, and learn from your actions. By learning, you build new skills and become a more valuable contributor to your organization. When you achieve exceptional results, you can be confident that they are an outcome of your actions rather than luck or circumstances.

Learn from your mistakes

If you make a mistake or have difficulty with a task, figure out why. This is different from assigning fault. Finding fault is a way to detach from or avoid accountability for the error. Analyzing the cause of the error will give you information you can use to correct the problem. When you have difficulty or make mistakes when completing a task, answer these questions to gain clarity:

- Are you motivated to do this task better? If not, why not?
- Do you know how to do the task? If not, what do you need to find out?
- Can you focus and concentrate on the task?
- What specific parts of the task do you have difficulty completing?
- Are you repeating the same errors?
- What seems to cause the errors?
- Have you tried to correct the problem? What helped? What didn't help?
- What else might you try to solve this problem?

For example, if you make calculation errors, start using a calculator or spreadsheet. If you are already using a calculator, change the kind of calculator you are using, slow down, or repeat your calculations twice to check for accuracy. If you make mistakes when you are distracted, reduce or remove distractions in the workspace. If you often make mistakes in a specific setting, come up with a long-term solution. If you always spill something at home, you put it in a different place or in a different container. Take a similar approach at work.

Success Story: I Can't Think Out Here

Here is an example of how analyzing errors can solve a performance problem. A woman with ISTJ personality preferences had problems entering data accurately. Her employer sent her to a performance coach to figure out why she was making so many errors. Together they analyzed her situation and found she often had to deal with interruptions, such as questions and phone calls, in the middle of data entry. She decided, with her employer's approval, to enter data on a computer in the back of the office when someone else was available to answer the phones and deal with the public. This small change helped her improve her accuracy.

Don't get caught up in a discussion about blame and fault when you make mistakes. Analyze what happened and fix it. Some of the more complex errors take time to analyze and understand. Ask for and listen to feedback to increase your awareness of your errors so you can understand and learn from them.

In most settings, trying things and making mistakes is a necessary part of learning and developing. A mistake usually becomes a problem only when you make it repeatedly and don't correct it. However, in some situations it isn't safe or prudent to try new things and take risks. Be aware of these limits when trying out new behaviors and testing solutions. Attempting new tasks and learning from mistakes does not mean you should engage in dangerous or unreasonable behaviors.

What about situations where I can't change anything?

Wait a minute, you say. When things go wrong, other people are sometimes to blame. You don't want to take responsibility for everyone's mistakes. True, everyone makes mistakes, and some situations are out of your control. Others sometimes can and do have an influence on your success and failure. However, you shouldn't use this as an excuse. Recognize tendencies to blame, trust luck, or deny your part in these situations. Recognize, too, that you may have played a part, however small, in what happened. In these cases you can still take ownership of and change your behaviors.

Part of taking ownership is determining what you can and cannot control. Then you can act on what is within your control. You can also take ownership for your reaction to what you can't control. You are responsible for how you react when others impede your ability to achieve results. For example, if someone is getting in the way of your progress, you may need to find alternative ways to accomplish your tasks. You may need to negotiate timelines if others are not delivering necessary resources.

Of course, you shouldn't hold yourself responsible for results that are out of your control. That will just cause undue stress. Do the best you can in a situation by accurately defining the limits of your control. You may need to negotiate or discuss the limits of your responsibility with others. In these cases, avoid blaming or complaining; simply explain your situation and limitations in a calm, reasonable discussion.

When possible, use your personal ownership to build your career success. Link the privileges and benefits you want from work to the responsibilities you are willing to take. Show others what you have accomplished. Your track record of accomplishments and personal responsibility pave the way for new opportunities.

For example, if you want to telecommute, assure your employer you will accomplish the same amount of work that would be done if you were working onsite. When looking for additional benefits, show your employer the logical links between accountability and privilege. Here are a couple of examples. If you want a raise, demonstrate how you add value to the company. If you want to enroll in a professional-development course, show how it will help you perform your work more effectively. Perhaps you can provide an example of how previous training enhanced your performance.

Do You Work Independently?

When you put yourself in charge, you accomplish your work independently. You decide what needs to get done next and take control of situations by taking action. When situations become problematic, you improve them. If you are an independent worker, you put in the necessary effort to achieve optimal results. Your coworkers are confident that you will complete every task or project you are assigned. Independent workers are appreciated and promoted in the workplace.

In the workplace, the general expectation is that people who understand the task at hand and have the skills and knowledge to do the work will carry out their duties independently. You may need to check in with a supervisor, peer, or leader in unusual circumstances or when faced with complicated problems or demands. Usually the employer will not see this as a problem. But you are expected to carry out your day-to-day tasks with no, or minimal, supervision or direction.

Individuals who don't work independently take up an employer's time and energy. They require frequent supervision and direction. If they don't get specific information about what to do next, they may simply stop working and wait to be told what to do. Dependent workers expect big results from a small amount of effort and are not willing to persist on tasks. Employers see dependent workers as helpless, passive, unwilling to attack or solve difficult problems, and reluctant to take action to improve their situation or achieve success. Employers will not promote or recommend workers who lack independence.

Working independently isn't the same thing as working alone. Independent workers regularly negotiate, delegate, communicate, and collaborate with others. Independent workers are in charge of their assignments and responsibilities and take on and complete tasks. They seek and use feedback to help them achieve their goals. If they need more information or direction, they get it.

It's possible to work *too* independently. You need to exercise the level of independence expected on the job—but no more. Making decisions on your own may interfere with the overall effort. You need to consult others before changing procedures that affect them. You should also beware of completing work others don't see as a priority or necessary, or of taking on tasks without informing coworkers. Others may duplicate your effort, or you may use resources on one project that others wanted to apply elsewhere. For these reasons, it is important to put checks and balances on the amount of independence you show. Link your efforts with the efforts of others. Ask yourself, "Where on the independence-involvement continuum do I need to be, and how can I get there?"

Excel Your Way: Tips for Personality Types

If you have a preference for Thinking (T), you may be more independent in your approach than those who have a preference for Feeling (F). If you also have a preference for Introversion (I), you prefer to work independently and may not actively seek feedback on progress. People with these preferences (IT) may be seen as overly independent. Remind yourself to check in periodically with others to ensure that your work is aligned with theirs.

If you have a preference for Feeling (F), you likely thrive on positive feedback and appreciate support and encouragement as you work. This is especially true if you also have a preference for Extraversion (E). Individuals with these preferences (EF) may ask for direction as a way of connecting and interacting and thus may come across as dependent. Curtail your need for interaction as necessary to avoid appearing dependent.

Reasons for not working independently

If you want to develop more independence at work, you first need to understand why you depend on others for direction. Perhaps you have developed the habit of learned helplessness. Maybe you are unsure about what to do or lack the skills you need for your work. Maybe your leader's work style encourages your dependence. Lack of confidence or need for approval may also make you appear dependent at work. Chapter 3 discusses confidence and need for approval. This chapter looks at the other reasons.

Learned helplessness

Some people have learned to take a passive approach. Experience has convinced them their actions will be ineffective, so they do not take any action. Statements such as "It won't do any good to try" or "It doesn't matter what I do" characterize this approach. Others just find it easier to ask and be directed than to figure things out for themselves. This approach allows them to avoid any sense of personal responsibility; they tell them-selves, "I was only doing what they told me to do."

If you are more comfortable being told what to do than working independently, you need to start asking yourself questions before you ask someone else. Rather than asking how to do something, first try to figure it out yourself. If you are unsure of which task to complete next, try to decide which task is more important. Anticipate what you should be doing. Make and share a list of your duties and ask for confirmation. In this way you begin to take charge rather than depending on others to decide for you. Find opportunities to discuss priorities and responsibilities with a supervisor or leader. Be active rather than passive in determining your roles.

> ## Excel Your Way: Tips for Sensing, Judging (SJ) and Intuitive (N) Types
>
> If you have a preference for Sensing and Judging (SJ) you may hesitate to act in-dependently when you are unsure of expectations or lack a clear understanding of the situation at hand. Clear, specific, and well-defined processes, procedures, and criteria for a decision help you maintain your independence at work. Ask for these or create them yourself if they are not available.
>
> If you have a preference for Intuition (N), it is easiest to work independently when you see how the tasks at hand relate to and contribute to larger goals or visions. Before acting independently, you want to see the implications and future results of your actions. Ask others to share the big-picture purposes for your ac-tions. If they do not have a vision, you may need to create one for yourself.

Not knowing what to do

You may be especially hesitant to take risks and work independently when you move into new roles and duties. When you are unfamiliar with a task, you may need information, training, supervision, reminders, evaluation, and feedback before you can tackle it independently. You gradually will become more independent in performing tasks as you develop confidence and competence.

Be sure you understand the scope of your work and the expected standards. When you are given new duties, confirm or clarify exactly what you are supposed to do. Record the information so you don't need to ask again. Explore training or resources you need to accomplish your tasks. This will allow you to feel comfortable with your new duties and establish competence.

Excel Your Way: Tips for Extraverted (E) and Introverted (I) Types

Extraverted (E) types may seek input as a way of thinking about and understanding a task. They are not necessarily seeking direction; rather, they are simply thinking out loud. However, this behavior can come across to others as somewhat needy or dependent. Let people know when you are thinking out loud, and try to use this behavior less frequently.

Introverted (I) types tend to reflect on situations and test the options before seeking input. They sometimes appear more independent. People with Introverted preferences may stop working on a task because they are unsure how to proceed. In these cases, if you can't figure out what to do, don't hesitate to ask for direction.

Leadership practices that discourage independence

Organizations may reinforce dependence by neglecting to give people authority to work independently within their scope. When you need to take action or make a decision, are you expected to check with your supervisor first? Or do you have the authority to act or decide on your own? In the latter case, do you have the tools, guidelines, processes, criteria, or procedures in place to act independently? You may want to discuss these questions with leaders in your organization. Remember to bring your opinions and possible solutions to the conversation; don't simply ask questions and passively await feedback.

Leadership style and practices can also greatly influence the amount of independence people demonstrate at work. Some supervisors and leaders are very directive in their leadership approach and discourage workers from acting autonomously. If leaders are interested in maintaining control and want workers to act in specific ways, workers are unlikely to respond to situations independently for fear of discipline. When leadership changes, workers often don't know what level of autonomy is expected of them. If the new leader has different expectations from the previous one, the workers' behaviors probably will not match up. Sometimes it is difficult to adjust to these changes. Observe your leader carefully to see how much independence he or she expects from you, and follow through by taking action and making decisions within the scope your leader expects. Having a discussion with your new leader can clarify his or her expectations.

Are You Persistent?

When you put yourself in charge of your success, you persist on tasks. When the task becomes complex and difficult, you stick with it until it is done. If you give up too easily, or try a number of things without a concentrated effort, you will likely be unsuccessful. Persistent people are resourceful, solution-oriented, and focused.

Some people struggle to persist; they quickly lose interest when tasks are routine and repetitive. Others become frustrated or tempted to give up on tasks that are highly complex, difficult, or challenging. That means tasks remain uncompleted and difficult problems remain unsolved. Check off items in the lists that follow to assess how persistent you are in your approach to work. Challenge yourself to increase your persistence.

Evidence of giving up easily

- ☐ Shifting focus from one task to another without completing the initial task
- ☐ Avoiding or procrastinating on certain tasks
- ☐ Becoming stuck or unable to proceed when there are barriers to progress

- ☐ Using an ineffective problem-solving approach
- ☐ Failing to follow through on obligations and responsibilities

Evidence of persistence

- ☐ Working on a task for an extended period
- ☐ Finding ways to maintain interest in tasks that don't motivate you
- ☐ Using resourcefulness to find ways around barriers
- ☐ Taking a systematic, problem-solving approach to problems
- ☐ Following through on obligations and responsibilities

Excel Your Way:
Tips for Judging (J) and Perceiving (P) types

If you have a preference for Judging (J), you are naturally focused on completing tasks and find it easy to follow through. However, you are less likely to persist on tasks that are not directly linked to a result. Try to ascertain whether your tasks are necessary.

If you have a preference for Perceiving (P), you naturally prefer to initiate rather than complete tasks. You may become bored with a task before completing it and switch to something else. You may find highly structured and routine tasks especially difficult to complete. Adopt strategies to enhance your follow-through.

Assessing your reasons for lack of persistence is the first step toward improvement. If you are unsure why you find it hard to persist on a task, start keeping track of the times when you want to give up. This will help you identify your barriers to persistence. The following sections discuss some common reasons for lack of persistence and some strategies to improve persistence.

Maintain your concentration and attention

Some people struggle to stay focused on tasks. This can be an enormous block to persistence. If you have trouble concentrating, develop strategies to help you focus on the task at hand. Here are some suggestions you can try.

- Notice what distracts you. Is it sights, sounds, sensations such as uncomfortable clothes or hunger, or distracting thoughts? After you identify the distractions, you can quickly notice when you are becoming distracted and when you need to refocus on the task.
- Vary your activities, take short breaks, and reward yourself for progress.
- Evaluate your workspace and experiment with changing the environment. For example, for some people, it's easier to concentrate with music than with silence. Music masks small sounds that might otherwise be distracting. Windows, hallways, and art on the wall are other possible sources of distraction.
- Minimize common distractions such as conversations with coworkers, phone calls, e-mail, and radio. Perhaps you can move to a different workspace, close your door, shut off your e-mail, or let voicemail take calls.
- Assess your physical readiness to work. Monitor hunger, fitness, time-of-day rhythms, and tension. Try to schedule tasks that require the most concentration for times when you are alert and energized.
- Assess whether personal issues are distracting you from your work. Do what you can to resolve minor problems. You need to deal with major problems outside the workplace. Consider seeking professional help if your personal problems are interfering with your work.
- Organize your workspace and resources to minimize the time you spend looking for things.
- If you are taking any medications, check with your doctor to assess side effects. Some medications can affect your ability to concentrate.

Reduce boredom

If you are bored or lack motivation, you will find it difficult to continue on tasks. Most people dislike some aspects of their work. They tend to be less persistent on these tasks and give them low priority. When people are not interested in the tasks they need to do, they can either do them anyway or change the type of work they are doing. Someone who is not suited to the work at hand is unlikely to become highly engaged or motivated.

Think about how engaged you are in your work. If you lack motivation, assess whether your current role is a good fit for you. If not, you may want to consider a career or role change.

Success Story: Sitting Isn't Fitting

Here is an example of how a worker's dislike for tasks can create a performance issue. A worker with ESTP personality type preferences was reassigned from warehouse work to data management after an injury. His work habits degenerated almost immediately. He was not used to sitting and did not like the highly detailed computer work. After completing a career-planning process, he described his preference for active, practical work with opportunities to be flexible and adaptable. He negotiated a move into a demonstration-based safety-training role. His performance immediately improved.

Excel Your Way: Tips for Extraverted (E) and Introverted (I) types

Individuals with a preference for Extraversion (E) tend to find it especially tedious to work with highly detailed and complex tasks. They seek variety and change.

Individuals with a preference for Introversion (I) can get bored when tasks are too simple; they don't feel engaged unless tasks offer some depth and complexity.

You can't always expect to find a perfect work match. And even the most ideal job will involve some tasks that are less interesting to you. Therefore, it's important to learn to persist on uninteresting tasks. Identify the tasks that are particularly uninteresting and find motives to complete them. Take frequent small breaks to reward yourself for accomplishing all or part of a task. Some people focus on the most uninteresting task first and get it over with—the worst-first approach. Others challenge themselves to do the task faster or better.

Deal with repetitive tasks

Some people respond poorly to repetitive tasks; others seek out and enjoy them. Someone who loses interest when doing repetitive tasks may begin to make errors or complete the work more slowly. Some simply abandon or avoid the repetitive aspects of their work.

When working on repetitive tasks, consider the tradeoff between speed and accuracy. Both are important. When you complete tasks quickly, you can get more done faster, but you are apt to make errors. People who work more slowly usually have lower error rates but also get less done in a fixed period. In a similar way, speed may affect how thoroughly you complete a task. Working slowly may enable you to do a more careful and thorough job.

Ideally, you will find a balance between quality and quantity. Assess your accuracy when doing routine tasks by counting the number of errors you make. Assess the importance of your errors and analyze their cause. This will help you determine the most appropriate balance between speed and accuracy. Work at a pace that results in the most reasonable standards for the quality and quantity of work you need to do.

When you must engage in highly repetitive tasks, you may need strategies to help you maintain your interest and accuracy. Look for opportunities to take breaks and engage in different types of tasks throughout the day. If you are doing repetitive physical tasks, pay attention to the ergonomics of the work setting so you can minimize the possibility of repetitive strain injuries.

Success Story: Dealing with the Details

The following example illustrates how people can learn to persist on and complete tasks not well suited to their personality. A woman with ENTP personality type preferences was working in a human resources office. She was responsible for a number of detailed, repetitive tasks, including data entry and verifying accuracy of data. She found these tasks uninteresting and had difficulty persisting on them. After some discussion with her leader, she got permission to add less detailed tasks to her workload. She balanced the time she spent on the tedious work with time spent focusing on more conceptual and stimulating tasks. Setting up this multitasking approach allowed her to pay attention to the detailed tasks, knowing she would soon switch to a more rewarding activity.

Excel Your Way:
Tips for Sensing (S) and Intuitive (N) types

If you have a preference for Sensing (S), you are likely comfortable with some repetition, as long as you can achieve practical results and do the task in a way that makes sense to you. Sensing types may get bored completing tasks that do not have immediate applications. Look for the practical benefits of persisting on a task.

If you have a preference for Intuition (N), you work in starts and stops. You may work hard at something for a while and then lose your inspiration. You sometimes find it hard to maintain interest in a task unless you can foresee meaningful long-term results.

Avoid getting stuck

People tend to lack persistence when faced with problems they don't know how to solve or obstacles they don't know how to deal with. If you do not have a good strategy for solving problems, you can get frustrated and give up. You may start to use a trial-and-error approach. Instead, try asking yourself these focusing questions to get unstuck: "What have I tried?" "What might be causing the problem?" "What can I try next?" These questions help you focus on solving the problem systematically. Problem-solving strategies are covered in depth in Chapter 8.

Even if you have good problem-solving strategies, you may not persist on a task if you lack essential skills or information. If this happens, make sure you have clear procedures to follow and reference materials such as process guidelines or standard operating procedures to help you. Seek learning activities to facilitate your ability to complete the task.

Sometimes, when your approach to a task or problem is not working, too much persistence can become an issue. In these cases, you must change course and try different strategies and approaches to accomplish your goals. Assess your work style. Do you need to be more persistent on tasks by concentrating your effort, or do you need to recognize when to change gears so you don't put in unproductive efforts? You succeed when you are persistent and resourceful at the right times.

Manage interruptions

Interruptions can be a barrier to persistence. Try dividing your work into interruptible and uninterruptible categories. Set up your workspace to facilitate working on uninterruptible tasks. For example, you may need to close the door, turn off the phone, and let others know you are unavailable for a specific period. When you can't block out interruptions, develop strategies for refocusing quickly. Look for simple ways to minimize interruptions. For example, maybe you can face your desk away from the hall if others tend to make eye contact and engage in conversation as they pass by. Review the suggestions earlier in this chapter for maintaining attention.

Putting Yourself in Charge: Personality Type Strengths and Challenges

All personality types can put themselves in charge. Every personality type has unique strengths and challenges aligned to their natural preferences. Read through the information on your personality type for suggestions specifically tailored to your natural way of working.

Responders (ESTP and ESFP)

As a Responder, you likely are comfortable taking independent action. Therefore, you may not be highly motivated to sit in meetings to discuss tasks and align your work to the work of others. Others may see you as a bit too independent; try checking in with them regularly to make sure you are on track. You may become distracted by interesting stimuli in your environment, and you tend not to persist on less interesting tasks, especially if they are routine or highly repetitive. Following through is of less interest to you than moving on to the next, more appealing task. To increase your persistence, find ways to be active while accomplishing tasks. Move around or take short breaks to improve your concentration.

Explorers (ENTP and ENFP)

As an Explorer, you are most motivated by thinking about different ways to do things and new things to do. Your need to think out loud and discuss these ideas with others may come across as dependence or lack of persistence. You may have several tasks going at once; you are more motivated to start a new project than to follow through on a project you have already started. To increase your persistence, challenge yourself to pick one task to finish. You can become blocked when you are not highly engaged in or excited about the task at hand. You may need to talk to others to see the purpose for the task. Allow yourself some time to imagine new possibilities, but refrain from taking action on these until you make significant progress on existing tasks. Prioritizing or eliminating some of your projects may also help you increase your persistence.

Expeditors (ESTJ and ENTJ)

As an Expeditor, you are self-reliant and comfortable taking charge and making decisions. You enjoy working independently. You expect others to be independent as well and you may critique unsatisfactory results. Others may feel you are blaming them. Because you are naturally focused on results, persisting on tasks is not usually a problem for you. But you may have trouble persisting and following through when others' efforts affect your results, especially if their work is not of high quality or is not completed in a timely fashion. In these situations, you may take over and do the work yourself. Although you'll get results in the short term, you may end up overloaded in the long term. To avoid such scenarios, take time to negotiate and clarify roles and responsibilities.

Contributors (ESFJ and ENFJ)

As a Contributor, you naturally take responsibility for achieving results. You want to ensure that everyone is actively contributing, and you check in often to see if everyone is on the same page. Although you are motivated by a desire to collaborate, others may see you as somewhat dependent. They may also misinterpret your efforts to build rapport and consensus. Keep this in mind, especially when working with Introverted (I) and Thinking (T) types who may be more interested in working autonomously. You are results oriented and tend to be persistent, but you may find it difficult to persist on tasks that rely heavily on impersonal, logical analysis. To motivate yourself, identify ways in which these tasks will benefit others.

Assimilators (ISTJ and ISFJ)

As an Assimilator, you tend to be self-directed, practical, and independent when you know what is expected. You may be less independent when you lack specific goals or directives. You sometimes avoid asking for assistance when you are stuck. In such situations, focus on getting input to identify and define your tasks, roles, and responsibilities. Assimilators tend to persist, seek closure, and follow through on tasks. In fact, you may tend to overpersist in some situations. Keep in mind that old ways of doing things don't always work in a new situation. Challenge yourself to try new ways of doing things when the tried-and-true ways are not working.

Visionaries (INTJ and INFJ)

As a Visionary, you naturally take responsibility for completing tasks. Others may see you as overly independent, especially at the early stages of a project, when you seek time alone to conceptualize and structure the work ahead. To correct this misperception, you may need to share your thoughts and plans with others. Ask for input rather than simply stating how you have decided to do things. Persisting on routine and highly detailed tasks may be especially tedious for you. To increase your persistence on these kinds of tasks, link them to broader goals and outcomes. Be aware that you often get distracted by a tendency to seek new and better ways of doing your work. Questioning the importance of the work tasks and goals themselves may also be distracting.

Analyzers (ISTP and INTP)

As an Analyzer, you are independent and self-reliant; you prefer to trust your own decisions and complete tasks alone. Others may see you as overly independent and even somewhat aloof. You may need to check in more often to make sure your work aligns with others' efforts. Motivated by the challenge of solving problems, you tend to be highly persistent when analyzing situations. However, your interest may quickly diminish when you have figured out the solution to a problem, so you may neglect to follow through. Others will not see your persistence if you don't implement the solution. You may find it especially difficult to persist when inefficient or illogical processes are involved.

Enhancers (ISFP and INFP)

As an Enhancer, you focus on your role in successes and failures. Because you want to ensure that your actions align with and support the needs of others, you may take more than your share of personal responsibility. You may even take responsibility for others' success. You also may defer your actions until you know what others want. Although your aim is to collaborate, support, and help others, coworkers may see you as somewhat dependent or passive. Carve out a space in your workday to achieve personal work goals and tasks. Then devote time to joint efforts and collaboration. Set boundaries to avoid taking on responsibility for others. You enjoy the startup phase of projects more than persisting on tasks. If you find it especially difficult to persist on impersonal tasks, try to link these tasks to personal values or benefits.

Reflection and Action

This chapter shows why it's essential to put yourself in charge. By taking responsibility for your actions, working independently, and persisting on tasks, you create your own career success. Are you taking charge of your career? Or do you tend to blame others and make excuses for your progress? Do you work independently and persistently? Review the checklists in the chapter and think about the suggestions offered. In the area below, write out some steps you can take to put yourself in charge.

CHAPTER FIVE

....

Learn from
Everyone

*L*earning from others is an essential part of your work. Other people provide you with information, instructions, and feedback and offer you a chance to learn about differing needs, opinions, and perspectives. When you take a learning approach to interacting with others, you are seen as diplomatic, empathic, understanding, tactful, nonjudgmental, open-minded, and considerate. Your interactions improve, and you develop a network of people who are interested in your progress and willing to help you develop your career.

When you listen to, and learn from, all the people around you, you invite new perspectives and develop rapport. Others sense your interest in listening and learning; they are encouraged to share new ideas and let you know about opportunities. Everyone has something to teach you.

Even people you find irritating or rude can teach you something, serving as examples of what you *don't* want to do. By observing how people interact and react, you can learn what is comfortable and appropriate. For example, groups of people—in the workplace, at home, and elsewhere—may tease, use sarcasm, share jokes, and lob putdowns. These types of communications may become accepted and expected within the group. However, newcomers, outsiders, and even some group members may find these types of communications uncomfortable.

Observe how the people around you communicate and note how people respond to communications and interactions. See what encourages and discourages people from continuing to interact and share their information and ideas. This will start you on the road to learning from others and thinking about what kinds of interactions are acceptable or unacceptable.

Are You Listening?

Listening is the key to learning from everyone. If you don't listen to what others say, they will be frustrated and dissatisfied when they interact with you. If you are seen as unreceptive to, or intolerant of, alternative views, your interactions may be filled with conflicts and unresolved issues. If you don't listen carefully you may misinterpret, reject, or ignore instructions, information, or feedback. No one is eager to interact with someone who appears uninterested, closed-minded, or critical. Employers value employees who listen carefully and respond to instructions and corrective feedback.

This chapter identifies ineffective listening habits and other problems that get in the way of listening to and learning from others, and provides tips and strategies for enhancing your listening. To listen and learn, you first need to *look* as if you are paying attention. You may argue that you can listen well even when you are text messaging or engaged in other tasks, and this may be true. But others want to see they have your attention. If they think you aren't focused on them, they may decide you are not interested in what they are saying.

Ineffective listening habits

Check off the ineffective listening habits you have from the following list. Strive to avoid these behaviors when you are listening. Here are some things *not* to do when you talk with others.

- ☐ Answer your phone
- ☐ Work on electronic devices
- ☐ Try to accomplish something else
- ☐ Fidget

- ☐ Rush in with comments whenever there is silence
- ☐ Interrupt
- ☐ Check the time
- ☐ Use physical space as a barrier (by sitting behind a large desk, for example)
- ☐ Sit with your arms or legs crossed
- ☐ Look away from the speaker frequently

Communication shutdowns

Your verbal responses also encourage or discourage others from communicating with you. Communication can shut down very quickly when listeners say the wrong thing. Communication shutdowns discourage others from expressing and elaborating on their views.

Read the following list of common communication stoppers. Check off the shutdown behaviors you use while listening and strive to avoid them.

Common communication shutdowns

- ☐ Diagnosing a problem, advising, or offering solutions rather than listening to concerns
- ☐ Labeling, criticizing, or evaluating the speaker's words or actions
- ☐ Arguing with the speaker's logic or debating the speaker's feelings
- ☐ Avoiding or ignoring the speaker's feelings or concerns
- ☐ Being unresponsive
- ☐ Being overly reassuring or sympathetic
- ☐ Being sarcastic, condescending or patronizing
- ☐ Pretending to understand when you really don't
- ☐ Defending your personal views or actions
- ☐ Breaking confidentility

Everyone uses some communication shutdowns. Sometimes these responses are appropriate or acceptable within certain groups or in certain types of communications. For example, at times it can be helpful to diagnose a problem or offer a solution. However, your goal is to learn from others by listening, and when you use any of these shutdown behaviors, speakers are likely to stop communicating. A communication shutdown is a lose-lose situation that can affect your career success.

Nobody wants coworkers or supervisors to moralize, preach, judge, or lay blame. You should always listen rather than challenge, at least until the speaker has had a chance to state his or her point. Avoid saying "I told you so" or asking "Why?" questions frequently. These responses tend to make speakers defensive. Your task is to listen and understand.

Success Story: I'm Right; You're Wrong

The following example shows how communication stoppers can affect work performance. An employee with INTJ personality type preferences had trouble being a team player because he couldn't accept decisions he considered illogical or less than optimal. In fact, his ideas and solutions were often much better than the team's decisions. But he was unable to persuade his team members to adopt his solutions because he did not show any interest in seeing their perspectives. He was only interested in showing them they were wrong. As a result, the team lost interest in his input. With some coaching, he learned to be more accepting and flexible, and his team members became much more receptive to his ideas.

Are You Encouraging Others to Teach You?

After you assess your use of ineffective habits and communication shutdowns, you can start to replace these behaviors with new ones that encourage others to talk to you. These communication encouragers are sometimes called *active listening strategies*. Good listeners don't just sit and listen; they actively show others they are engaged and interested. Good listeners suspend their beliefs and curb their responses as they strive to understand others' perspectives. They are nonjudgmental and considerate when listening. When given information, including feedback, they clarify and act on it.

Excel Your Way: Tips for Extraverts (E) and Introverts (I)

If you have a preference for Extraversion (E), you may tend to interrupt and finish other people's sentences. Although you are anticipating what the person plans to say or adding to the conversation, others can find this behavior annoying and may shut down communications. Wait until the other person is finished before you speak.

If you have a preference for Introversion (I), you may focus internally when you are listening and may not show a lot of outward expression. As a result, others may think you are not listening. Practice using nonverbal cues to show you are listening.

Effective listening habits

To listen effectively, you must first encourage others to share information with you. Use the list below to check off the active listening strategies you are already using.

- ☐ Turning off distracters such as the computer, telephone, or other electronic devices
- ☐ Leaning forward attentively
- ☐ Keeping your own talk to a minimum
- ☐ Nodding or tilting your head
- ☐ Using eye contact (without staring or being intimidating)
- ☐ Providing a comfortable personal space
- ☐ Keeping a positive expression and stance

Success Story: What Are You Thinking?

Speakers look for cues from listeners to help them gauge reactions. The following example illustrates difficulties that arise when a speaker is not receiving cues.

A man with INFP personality type preferences proved almost impossible for colleagues to read. When others shared information, he responded with a blank face; he didn't nod or use any other active listening cues. When challenged on this behavior, he replied that he had been actively listening to and thinking about the information. He realized, however, that he had not put any energy into acknowledging others' input. His working relationships improved when he began to focus outward and demonstrate interest and enthusiasm when coworkers spoke.

Encouragers

You can encourage communication by making short comments or asking brief questions that show interest and invite the speaker to continue. Such listening encouragers can feel artificial and contrived until you get used to them. It takes practice and feedback to encourage others to communicate. Try using some of the following encouragers.

- What happened then?
- What did you do then?
- How did that turn out?
- Tell me more.
- Oh no!

Summaries

When you encourage others to share information, demonstrate that you want to learn from and understand what the speaker is saying. One simple technique is to summarize what you hear. Of course, your summary should relate directly to what the speaker is saying. Here are a few examples of how listeners can summarize part of a conversation to show they understand and are engaged in listening.

- That guy wouldn't give up, would he?
- Sounds like you're swamped with work.
- Every time you turned around, you ran into another problem.
- I'm hearing you really would like some help with this.

Excel Your Way: Tips for Judging (J) and Perceiving (P) Types

If you have a preference for Judging (J), you like coming to closure, and you may find it easier to summarize than to encourage. Practice using encouraging statements to show you are listening in an open-ended manner.

If you have a preference for Perceiving (P), you naturally enjoy open-ended discussions and may find encouraging easier than summarizing. Practice making summary statements to show you understand the speaker's viewpoint.

Confirm what you heard

It's easy to know when your summary is on target; the speaker will say something like "Exactly" or "That's for sure." When your summary is off base, the speaker will let you know right away, either by disagreeing or disengaging. At this point, try to find out what the speaker *did* mean. When someone gives you new information, summarize to make sure you heard it correctly. Summarizing what you hear also helps you remember it.

Use a check statement and then summarize the message. Good check statements include

- I want to make sure I understand . . .
- Let me make sure I got all of that correctly . . .
- I heard . . . . Is that right?

Check statements and summaries, like encouragers, can seem artificial at first; you may feel as if you are simply parroting back what you hear. The awkward feeling diminishes with practice. These behaviors are powerful tools for clarifying and enriching communications.

Excel Your Way:
Tips for Thinking (T) and Feeling (F) Types

If you have a preference for Thinking (T), you may dismiss the idea of making summary statements because restating the obvious seems like a waste of time. However, these statements encourage the speaker to continue and help you ensure that you are interpreting accurately. For these reasons it is worth taking time to practice summary statements, especially when communicating with Feeling (F) types.

If you have a preference for Feeling (F), you may use encouragers and summary statements regularly. You may even use them too frequently, making others impatient. Assess each situation. Sometimes it is better to move ahead and cover new ground rather than validate others. This may be especially true in highly task-focused communications with Thinking and Judging (TJ) types.

Don't be afraid that listening to and accepting someone else's perspective indicates that you endorse it. The point of encouraging others to express their views is to listen and understand. Hearing and understanding a person's opinion does not mean you agree with it. Rather, it provides a starting point for further discussion.

Listen first, and then demonstrate that you understand what was said. If necessary, you can disagree after the speaker is finished and knows he or she has been heard. Too many dead-end conversations consist of two people explaining and reiterating their own perspectives because neither has acknowledged having heard and understood what the other is saying.

Are You Being Empathic?

When you respond empathetically, you encourage others to communicate. Empathic responses are the opposite of communication shutdowns—the types of responses that discourage others from expressing themselves. Empathic responses are nonjudgmental; they acknowledge the feelings underlying the speaker's words.

Empathic responses demonstrate the listener's consideration and compassion for the speaker and are important for establishing rapport and building relationships with others. People show consideration any time they listen to others and attempt to understand their perspectives. But empathic responses go further, actively encouraging others to express their views. To provide an empathic response, you must try to imagine what it is like to be in a certain situation or to experience a certain feeling. However, avoid telling the speaker you know *exactly* how he or she feels.

It is sometimes difficult to see the difference between empathy and sympathy. Empathetic comments and actions demonstrate an understanding and appreciation of another person's situation. Empathy is the ability to see a situation from the other person's perspective. Sympathetic comments tend to express regret and sorrow about someone's situation or plight.

It is appropriate to express sympathy when someone experiences a loss. In other situations, sympathy can come across as condescending and even deprecating. People generally don't want to hear comments with a "poor you" or "I feel so sorry for you" tone. They want to be understood and acknowledged, not pitied.

Empathic responses

Empathetic responses validate the speaker's viewpoint; they show you are listening and trying to understand his or her perspective. Such responses are similar to, but go beyond, summary statements by reflecting back the emotional tone of the speaker. Empathy encourages the speaker to continue sharing information and helps you learn from his or her experiences. When you first attempt such responses, you may think you sound stilted and insincere. Assess your efforts by noting how people respond to your comments. If possible, rehearse communication encouragers and empathic responses with a peer or coach. Here are some examples of empathetic responses.

- I imagine that must have been very frustrating for you.
- It sounds like that would be very discouraging.
- I bet you were steaming mad when that happened.

Is empathy always necessary?

Empathy is not always the most appropriate response in the workplace. At times it is more important to get to the task at hand, provide corrective feedback, or discuss solutions to a problem.

Excel Your Way: Tips for Thinking (T) and Feeling (F) Types

Thinking (T) types may not always see logical reasons for accommodating others in the workplace. Devote more time and energy to building relationships and understanding the people around you. If you don't, you may alienate and lose the cooperation of some of the people you need to work with.

Feeling (F) types are naturally attracted to accommodating others in the workplace. Be aware that not all individuals are interested in "small talk" and developing rapport at work. You may need to limit the amount of time you spend building and nurturing work relationships.

Tensions can arise between those who prefer work relationships to be mostly impersonal and task-oriented and those who want to establish rapport and build relationships. These tensions tend to align with preferences for Feeling and Thinking. Feeling types are interested in establishing personal relationships with coworkers and are naturally attuned to understanding and thinking about others' perspectives. Thinking types usually want to keep work relationships focused on work matters. However, everyone benefits by listening actively and considering alternative viewpoints; these behaviors are essential to career success.

Success Story: Point Not Taken

The following example shows how listening can solve problems and enhance work performance. A construction supervisor with the personality type ISFP was concerned about the sub-trade workers' decreasing morale because they were working long hours and weekends. The ESTJ manager was concerned about results because projects were behind schedule. Neither one initially listened to the other's concerns, although the solution was in the listening. After the supervisor and the manager acknowledged each other's concerns, the solution was easy. The manager relaxed the timelines somewhat, and workers got some breaks. Immediately morale improved and the workers became more productive. Soon construction projects got back on schedule.

Are You Clarifying Expectations?

While active listening and empathic responses provide a good start to establishing rapport and ensuring that others are comfortable expressing alternative opinions, you also need to clarify and act on what others say. Clarification goes beyond listening to and accepting someone's perspective; it also means focusing on what the speaker might expect or need from you.

Why people communicate

People communicate for a number of reasons. Sometimes they simply want to share their perspective. More frequently, though, speakers want the listener to respond by doing something, such as following directions, fulfilling expectations, or providing assistance. The speaker may be seeking information or clarification, or providing feedback. Active listeners confirm what they hear and check to see if there are more points the speaker would like to add. When you clarify and act on communication, you learn new information, change your course of action, and determine the best way to accomplish a task.

When clarifying a communication, focus on the purpose behind the communication—without being overly sensitive, suspicious, analytical, or critical. When listening, mentally assess what the reasons for this particular communication might be so you can respond appropriately. Then you can clarify, confirm, and act on the message. The following list provides a number of reasons people communicate in the workplace.

- To share an emotion
- To complain about other people or circumstances
- To share information or an opinion
- To express enthusiasm and build support for actions or ideas
- To report a change that will affect you
- To convince you of something
- To make you sensitive to or aware of something
- To get your input, opinion, or feedback

- To give you directions or instructions
- To ask you to take action or solve a problem
- To give you positive feedback or corrective feedback
- To ask you to make a decision
- To solicit information, assistance, or support
- To connect with and learn more about you
- To persuade you to change your opinion
- To get your agreement on an issue
- To align with you (perhaps for or against something or someone)
- To impress you
- To think out loud

How to Clarify

When you respond to others, your response must align to the purpose of the communication. Your task is to make sure you heard what you were supposed to hear. Sometimes you can easily determine the speaker's purpose; other times it's less obvious, and you must seek clarification.

It can be tricky to clarify the purpose of a communication without coming across as challenging, probing, or doubting. Start internally. Try to figure out why the speaker wants to talk to you about this topic. Look at the situation from his or her perspective. Assume the person is acting with good intentions (unless you have powerful reasons to think otherwise). Listen carefully to the speaker's words and observe his or her body language.

Then check in with the speaker. Explore—diplomatically—his or her purpose. If you think the speaker wants you to complete a task, ask for details such as where, when, and how the task needs to be done. If the speaker is looking for information, find out exactly what and how much data you need to find. Checking in tells the speaker that you understand the purpose of the communication, and it ensures that you receive all the details you need to respond appropriately. As you clarify the communication, you are also clarifying expectations and making sure your actions align with the expectations.

Excel Your Way: Tips for Sensing (S) and Intuitive (N) Types

If you have a preference for Sensing (S), you naturally clarify facts and details. Challenge yourself to clarify the speaker's overall objective as well. Others may want to know that you see their purpose or vision.

If you have a preference for Intuition (N), you naturally clarify general purposes and objectives. Challenge yourself to clarify the facts and details as well. Others may want to know that you understand the important realities and practicalities of the situation.

When you misinterpret communications, you are bound to respond inappropriately. For example, if someone simply wants to express an emotion, offering a solution is not a helpful response. If someone wants you to take action, simply agreeing with their point of view and not acting will frustrate them. Clarifying communications and expectations helps prevent these kinds of problems.

Success Story: What Do You Want from Me?

Here is an example that demonstrates the importance of understanding the speaker's purpose. A woman with ENTJ personality type preferences described the following communication dilemma with an ENFP coworker. When the ENFP discussed problems with the ENTJ, the ENTJ offered a solution. Then the ENFP became frustrated; she said she didn't want a solution and felt the ENTJ was being condescending by giving "the answer" to her. The ENFP simply wanted to air the problem, think it through, and consider possibilities. After the ENFP defined the purpose for the communication, the ENTJ became less solution-oriented during their discussions. The ENFP also learned to clarify what she was looking for in interactions.

Are You Learning from Corrective Feedback?

Corrective feedback is one of the more difficult interactions to learn from. But feedback is a powerful tool for self-improvement. You can use it to stimulate your thinking about how to improve your work and perform your tasks more effectively. As well, everyone has blind spots—weaknesses outside our awareness. Corrective feedback can start you thinking about how to develop areas you hadn't considered before. While we can all benefit from corrective feedback, many people are unwilling to listen to or learn from others and may respond by discarding, denying, or arguing with what they are hearing.

Excel Your Way: Tips for Thinking (T) and Feeling (F) Types

If you have a preference for Thinking (T), you can be self-critical and quick to point out your own flaws. However, you may ignore feedback that is not in line with your self-assessment. This can be especially true if the feedback strikes you as illogical or if you suspect the individual providing feedback is not highly credible and competent. Challenge yourself to take time to consider what is being said, and why, before you dismiss what you hear. This will help you learn more from the situation.

If you have a preference for Feeling (F), you may be more focused on appreciating and validating than on critiquing. When others provide corrective feedback, you may take it as a personal affront and become upset. It can be a challenge to accept feedback, especially if it is given in a frank and impersonal manner. Remember that corrective feedback about your actions is not a critique of your worth as a person. Work toward interpreting feedback as an effort to help you improve rather than as a personal attack.

When receiving feedback, you need to respond in an objective and open-minded way. This can be a challenge, especially if you feel threatened, incompetent, or unappreciated. Sometimes it can be difficult to admit mistakes. These personal reactions come across as defensive responses, disbelief, arguments, disengagement, or disappointment. You need to recognize these unproductive reactions to feedback and learn to set aside your personal responses so you can listen without making an overly emotional retort.

Unhelpful responses to feedback

Read the following list of unhelpful responses to feedback and check off any statements that describe how you typically respond.

- ☐ Arguing with the feedback
- ☐ Reacting emotionally or personally to the information
- ☐ Dismissing or undervaluing feedback
- ☐ Interrupting or changing the subject
- ☐ Blaming others rather than acknowledging your part in the situation
- ☐ Continuing to engage in behaviors for which you received negative feedback

Learn to react effectively to feedback. First, check to make sure you understand the feedback. You may need to ask for more information. Do this without argument or debate.

Next, acknowledge what you heard. When you acknowledge feedback, focus on not reacting defensively—the whole purpose is to understand what the other person has said, not to explain your behavior or to elaborate on reasons for it. Accept that the person giving the corrective feedback does see the behavior in question as a problem. That is their reality. Denying someone else's reality creates additional conflict or disagreement.

After you have heard and acknowledged the feedback, thank the speaker for giving it. At times, you may need to concede that you made a mistake or acted inappropriately, or acknowledge that your actions have offended or created difficulty for others. Apologize for any inappropriate actions. When you apologize, do it unconditionally. Avoid statements that begin, "I'm sorry, but—." In general, apologies are most effective when they are short, specific, and sincere.

Do not comment on the feedback until you have listened to and acknowledged it. At this point, if it seems appropriate to disagree with the feedback, do so in a calm, objective manner. Share your alternative perspective in a way that makes sense to, and shows appreciation for, the person who gave the feedback.

After you receive feedback, consider what you learned from the experience and how you can use this information to improve your performance. After you take action to improve, check to ensure that your actions have the desired effect.

Steps for accepting corrective feedback

Here is a summary of the process you can use to incorporate corrective feedback. Check off the steps you are using now and target steps you can improve on when you receive feedback.

- ☐ Listen carefully to what is being said using active-listening behavior.
- ☐ React calmly and objectively.
- ☐ Reiterate, acknowledge, and clarify what you heard.
- ☐ Thank the speaker for the feedback.
- ☐ Assess whether it would be helpful to apologize, and if so, give a short, specific, and sincere apology.
- ☐ Assess whether you need to share your perspective at all, and if so, speak in a respectful manner.
- ☐ Think about, and make a decision about, what to do in response to the feedback.
- ☐ Take appropriate action as a result of the feedback.

Learning from Everyone: Personality Type Strengths and Challenges

All personality types can learn from each other. Every personality type has unique strengths and challenges aligned to their natural preferences. Read through the information on your personality type for suggestions specifically tailored to your natural way of working.

Responders (ESTP and ESFP)

Responders may find it difficult to listen without interrupting. You are action-oriented and often want to *do* something rather than discuss matters in detail. Others may believe you are not listening when you engage in other tasks while they speak, and they may interpret your need for action as impatience or a lack of interest. Use active listening strategies, especially those that help you focus on the interaction, and avoid distracters. Listen to everything a speaker says and then clarify and summarize priorities; don't simply listen to part of the communication and then jump into action.

Explorers (ENTP and ENFP)

Explorers can become distracted by ideas and possibilities. You may find yourself sharing, connecting, and expanding ideas rather than listening carefully to what is being said. Eager to express your thoughts, you may have trouble listening without interrupting. Practice your active listening skills. Create a framework or an overview to help you listen and understand when others present facts and details. There is a time and place for brainstorming, building on ideas, and imagining, but these activities do not promote listening and understanding. To improve your listening, summarize and clarify what others say before you add your thoughts.

Expeditors (ESTJ and ENTJ)

As an Expeditor, you are task– and goal-oriented. You may become impatient when others spend workplace time developing personal relationships. Remember that some people will be more productive and willing to work with you when you take time to develop rapport and demonstrate empathy. Listen without interrupting. Pay attention, and learn to avoid communication shutdowns such as offering solutions or advising. You may see these forms of communication as logical and effective. However, they can keep you from working effectively with, and learning from, others.

Contributors (ESFJ and ENFJ)

Contributors seek to understand people's values, opinions, and reactions and usually find it easy to develop rapport and build relationships. You may struggle to listen when the information has a negative effect on others or is presented in an impersonal or overly frank manner. In these cases, focus on the content and the logic of the message. You will have time later to look at the personal side. Similarly, consider the value of corrective feedback as a learning tool for personal development. Accept that others do not always want to work on relationships, build morale, or discuss their personal lives at work, and accommodate this different approach.

Assimilators (ISTJ and ISFJ)

When Assimilators communicate with other types, they may process the information internally and may not show their engagement in a form others can recognize. You may be listening carefully, but others may not recognize this. Demonstrate your attention by using nonverbal and verbal cues such as nodding your head or using communication encouragers. Sequence and organize new information so you can process and understand it. Ask for clarification when you are presented with global, abstract, or unstructured information. Also ask for concrete examples and clear direction when others provide you with corrective feedback.

Visionaries (INTJ and INFJ)

Visionaries are big-picture thinkers who focus on complex concepts and theories rather than facts and details. When listening, you may be distracted by your efforts to align what is being said to what you know and understand about a given topic. Others may sense you are not interested in listening because they can't observe your reflections. You may need to show some listening cues through body language and encouragers. You may also become distracted from listening when you are presented with numerous unconnected facts and details. To clarify what you are hearing, ask for an overview, or try to organize the information into a summary.

Analyzers (ISTP and INTP)

Analyzers deal with almost any communication in a calm and objective manner. However, others can interpret this objectivity as a lack of interest or involvement. You prefer to analyze and critique situations, and you may become impatient with small talk, developing rapport, and sharing feelings. Find logical reasons for engaging in these behaviors. Watch out for a tendency to use sarcasm or cynicism as well as arguing, debating, and challenging when interacting. Although you mean no harm and get enjoyment from these forms of interactions, other types may respond negatively to them.

Enhancers (ISFP and INFP)

Enhancers are comfortable establishing rapport. You usually are open to learning from others, and you approach communication in a personal, appreciative way. Because you internalize your responses, others may not know how you feel. Use body language to show your reactions. You sometimes personalize what is being said and may find it difficult to listen objectively, especially when the information presented challenges important values. This can also make it difficult for you to hear corrective feedback. Strive first to hear and clarify the content of the communication; sort out your personal responses after the interaction.

Reflection and Action

This chapter shows why you need to learn from everyone. When two people carefully listen to each other—by using active listening skills, responding empathically, clarifying communications, and accepting corrective feedback—they both learn. Do you learn from everyone? Look at your responses to the checklists in the chapter and think about the suggestions offered. In the area below, write out some steps you can take to improve your ability to learn from everyone.

CHAPTER SIX

Relate to Anyone

Everyone needs to interact in order to do their work. Perhaps you interact with the general public, customers, clients, coworkers, or supervisors. You also interact with a variety of people who provide you with products and services. These interactions give you an opportunity to make connections and build a network of people who know you and your work.

This network of contacts can be a key resource for building your career. Your network can help you achieve your goals, improve your work performance, and explore new work options. Your network can support you and link you to other people. You can, in turn, support others and create strong and effective working relationships.

To relate to anyone, you need to communicate effectively. When you communicate effectively, others see you as amicable, cooperative, articulate, pleasant, and straightforward. When you relate to anyone, you promote teamwork and can complete your work more efficiently. When you express yourself well, people enjoy interacting with you and find it easy to listen to what you have to say.

As an effective communicator, you take time to think about and plan what you want to say and write. You customize your message and target it so others understand your purpose and content. When relating to others, you tactfully provide both positive and corrective feedback so they can learn from their successes and identify areas for improvement. You resolve conflicts and issues diplomatically so you can continue to collaborate and cooperate with others.

Are You Sending a Clear Message?

If you send confusing or unclear messages, people may misunderstand and misinterpret your meaning, and your information, feedback, or opinion may be lost in translation. If you neglect to think before you speak, you also run the risk of saying something you'll regret. Sometimes spur-of-the-moment communications, especially those that occur in emotional situations, can be overly harsh or cutting. You may come across as defensive, judgmental, argumentative, pretentious, domineering, or even aggressive. By planning what to say before sending your message, you can eliminate many of these communication problems.

Plan what to say

When you want to get important information across to others, plan ahead to ensure that your message will be well received. Thinking about and screening your words before you communicate helps you organize your thoughts, increases the effectiveness of your message, and makes miscommunication unlikely.

Excel Your Way:
Tips for Extraverts (E) and Introverts (I)

If you have a preference for Extraversion (E), you may naturally share whatever thoughts and emotions come to mind. Others tend to know where you stand on issues. However, they may tune you out if you speak too freely and without forethought. Sharing thoughts that are not well formulated leads to misinterpretation and foot-in-mouth experiences. Challenge yourself to think twice before speaking.

If you have a preference for Introversion (I), you naturally tend to think before you speak and you may not share information or opinions unless you see a reason to do so. This communication style reduces foot-in-mouth problems, and other people are likely to recognize the careful, well-thought-out nature of your communications. However, you might miss opportunities for valuable input. Not speaking up may also result in unresolved conflicts. In some situations, you may benefit from speaking up more.

Of course, it's impractical to carefully think about and plan every word you speak or write. However, you will benefit from putting some filters in place before you communicate. It is especially important to plan your communication when the information you are sharing may not be well received, or when it requires action. You should also develop a communication plan when you are going to provide a significant piece of feedback, make a major request or recommendation, or share other important information. To improve your communications, plan what you want to say and how you need to say it. A communication plan isn't a written document; it is a mental process that involves thinking about the best way to express what you want to say.

Decide what you want to communicate, and then consider your audience and how receptive they will be to the message. People have different preferences for taking in information, so consider how much and what type of information to provide. Some listeners want to hear all the details; others are more interested in a general overview. Some respond well to a personal, encouraging approach. Others are more interested in a logical, objective communication. Some prefer formal, written communications; others prefer information that is presented informally. Think about how to use relevant language; consider how to avoid overwhelming others with too much information (or confusing them with too little information), or intimidating them with jargon or unfamiliar words. Good communicators tailor each message to the needs of the listener.

Excel Your Way:
Tips for Judging (J) and Perceiving (P) Types

If you have a preference for Judging (J), you naturally share conclusions and decisions and discuss steps for accomplishing goals. Perceiving types may interpret your communications as directive or confining. Challenge yourself to postpone decisions and conclusions until everyone has a chance to consider the options.

If you have a preference for Perceiving (P), you naturally are comfortable with open-ended, free-flowing discussions and like to leave your options open. When communicating with Judging types (J), avoid presenting multiple options. Challenge yourself to focus on what is important and reach closure on a topic sooner than you might choose to.

Many people are so focused on sharing their thoughts, opinions, and ideas that they forget to think about how their message will be received, or whether it's a good idea to speak at all. Learning when you should *not* say anything is as important as learning how to say something. Ask yourself, "What do I want to say?" and "Why do I want to say it?" If the purpose of the communication is to make you feel better about something, and the information is not particularly helpful for the listener, perhaps you shouldn't say anything. On the other hand, you shouldn't refrain from communicating feelings, thoughts, or reactions that influence your working relationships. Determining how much to communicate is an important first step when planning your communication.

Here is a sample of useful questions to consider when planning your message. Of course, you can't think through all of these questions before every communication. However, this comprehensive list provides a starting point for improving your messages.

- Who is your audience—specifically, who are you communicating with?
- What, exactly, do you want to communicate?
- Why do you need to communicate this?
- How much time do you need?
- How can you customize the message to make sure the listener understands?
- Is the listener likely receptive to this message? How can you present the message so the listener will be more receptive?
- Does the message have emotional components? If so, how will you manage them? Have you considered the words you need to use to be objective about this topic?
- What is the best time and place for this message?
- How might your audience respond to this message? How will you handle these responses?

Answering these questions will help you think about and plan for important communications. Decide which questions are most important for the situation at hand.

It sounds tedious to go through this process every time you share information, thoughts, or feelings; however, it will become automatic with practice. There's no need to write down or mull over all the questions every time. Your goal is to send purposeful, effective, and targeted messages. By planning your communications, you can avoid potential conflicts and misunderstandings. Rehearsing an especially important or difficult communication with a friend or colleague can help you make sure you get your message across.

Success Story: Fitting In

Here is an example of how important it is to focus on others when communicating. A woman with ESFJ personality type preferences began working in a new setting. Her coworkers were quiet and worked harmoniously. She was friendly, outgoing, and interested in discussing personal issues and interpersonal relationships. She thought she was building rapport and relationships, but others found her overly direct and intrusive. When she received this feedback, the ESFJ worker started to pay more attention to the office environment. She noticed that the office was quiet and calm whenever she was not initiating communications. She realized she needed to tone down her interactions and let others work together peacefully.

Send effective messages

The following statements show you how to send clear, customized messages. Check off the techniques you are currently using and consider ways to incorporate the others in your daily communications.

To send clear messages

☐ State the purpose for the communication up front
☐ State why the communication is important
☐ Present well-organized information that stays on topic
☐ Explain the information clearly and succinctly
☐ Provide an overview as well as some concrete facts or details
☐ Answer questions and clarify content
☐ Adjust vocabulary and jargon to the audience
☐ Look for cues to assess how well others understand what is being said
☐ Ensure that the information is important and relevant

Success Story: Getting the Details Right

Sharing information can be difficult when the target audience or type of message is different from the sender's own preferences. Here is how one Intuitive (N) type described his team's strategy for getting the details right. "Part of our work role is to write technically detailed requirements and specifications documents for our clients' software implementations. These clients are very unhappy if there are any errors in the documents. Our account managers who are Sensing (S) types tend to excel in this role, especially the two ISTJ managers—they are stars at this. On the other hand, the account managers who prefer Intuition (N) usually find this task difficult and painful, but they know it is essential for successful communication. They tend to use coping behaviors, such as having another colleague double-check their work to ensure that the documents are accurate and detailed enough."

Consider your listener

When you express yourself, be aware of your audience's body language cues; they help indicate whether your listeners understand and are interested in what you have to say. When people become restless or uninterested, they tend to fidget, look puzzled, glance around the room, or start to do other activities. If people don't like the message they are hearing, they may frown, avoid eye contact, or cross their arms. Rather than simply plowing ahead with your communication, stop speaking and ask for input or questions to ensure that your message is being received. No matter how interesting and important the message is to you, if your listener is not receiving it, you aren't communicating effectively.

People are often unaware of how a comment or tone of voice affects others. Often, others may misinterpret comments that seem innocuous to you. Consider your listeners when communicating and present messages in a way they can understand. The listeners' personality preferences, learning style, background knowledge, interests, and values all affect the way in which they prefer to receive messages. Review the eight personality type descriptions at the end of this chapter for an overview of some common personality differences in communication. When you get to know individuals, you can communicate with them more effectively.

Excel Your Way:
Tips for Thinking (T) and Feeling (F) types

If you have a preference for Thinking (T), you likely enjoy debating and critiquing information and ideas. At times, others may misinterpret these interactions as personal attacks. Using a more diplomatic approach when interacting helps you develop rapport and work more effectively with Feeling (F) types.

If you have a preference for Feeling (F), you likely enjoy conversations focused on personal interests and values. Others sometimes find such personal conversations intrusive or irrelevant. Knowing when to shift away from pleasantries and attend to the task at hand improves your working relationships with Thinking (T) types.

Think about your relationship with the listeners and consider whether your message might take them by surprise. Perhaps you are often the bearer of bad news, or perhaps you didn't build a relationship with your listener before offering corrective feedback. In these situations, getting your message across effectively may be especially tricky.

Success Story: Flavor of the Month

A human resources manager with INTP personality type preferences had just started a new job. He quickly grew frustrated discussing change with his staff, many of whom had ISTJ personality preferences. No matter what approach he tried, they seemed to ignore his messages. After a few frank discussions with his staff, he discovered the organization had a history of introducing new initiatives with little support and follow-through. As a result, the initiatives usually failed. The employees learned to ignore change and made comments such as "This, too, shall pass." He found he needed to be more specific in his communication. When he demonstrated how the change would be implemented and supported, the staff finally took him seriously and began to hear what he had to say.

Choose an appropriate time and setting for communicating. What is appropriate, of course, depends on the purpose of the communication. Teaching a skill may be appropriate in one setting; sharing information about an organizational change or providing feedback may be better suited to a different setting. Make sure you have enough time to complete a communication before you start it, and avoid sharing important information in distracting settings. Respect privacy and confidentiality.

General communication tips

Be specific, honest, direct, and sincere when stating your message. Speak clearly and concisely, moderating your voice so that it is neither too quiet nor too loud. Don't expect others to pick up your points by mind reading. Communicate directly; avoid hinting at information rather than stating it clearly. Most of all, walk your talk. You lose credibility if you talk one way and act another. You need to do what you say you will do.

When expressing emotions, take ownership of them; don't assign blame or attribute your emotions to others. Consider these two statements: "You upset me when you don't listen"; "I feel upset when I think I am not being heard." People are much more likely to take the first statement personally. These nuances may seem trivial, but the way you express your personal feelings has a significant influence on the way the listener responds.

Find a balance between enthusiasm and calmness. When you present information in a calm, objective way, you minimize negativity. Certainly we have all experienced the destructiveness of negative comments made in highly charged moments. On the other hand, if you present information or respond to others *too* calmly, you may give the impression that you are unenthusiastic, detached, or uninterested.

When you show enthusiasm for a topic, your commitment and interest can inspire others. If you are overly enthusiastic, however, others may think you are overstating your point, trying to "sell" your ideas, or being idealistic. When balancing enthusiasm and calmness, consider the listener; thinking about your audience will help you give your message the right tone.

Also balance humor and seriousness when communicating. Humor can be an uplifting addition to communication. Laughter is energizing, and in some situations it can cut through tension. However, people have different ideas about what is funny, and they have different levels of tolerance for humor. As well, humor can be cutting and may poke fun at certain groups or individuals. Humor takes time, and others may become frustrated if you persist in responding humorously when they are attempting to address an important issue.

Taking a serious approach in your communications emphasizes the importance of a topic. Adopting a serious tone makes sense when you are discussing important issues, making decisions, and planning actions. In other situations, an overly serious tone can be off-putting. It can increase tension levels and suppress people's creative ideas. Those who are habitually serious may be at a loss during open-ended discussions, in which people use humor to encourage brainstorming. Consider whether you tend to be more humorous or serious in your approach and decide if you might benefit from balance in this area.

Teaching others

At times you may teach others or provide them with information or instructions. Instructing others is a specialized form of communication that requires additional planning. Here are some points for presenting information effectively in front of a group.

- Focus on your learners—who are they and what do they need to know?
- Evaluate background knowledge—find out what your learners already know.
- State what you plan to accomplish and explain up front why learners need to know this information.
- Prepare your ideas and gather all the facts you need before you begin.
- Come prepared with data, examples, principles, and logic to back up your information.
- Accommodate your learners' interest levels and learning styles.
- Share expert information at levels and in quantities the learners can retain.
- Provide written or visual aids.
- Avoid telling people what to do unless absolutely necessary. Many people resist this.
- When you need to give direction, be clear, specific, and concise.
- Check for understanding without being condescending.

- Anticipate and prepare for questions or criticisms.
- Answer questions in a direct, clear, and organized way.
- If you don't know, say so.

Excel Your Way: Tips for Sensing (S) and Intuitive (N) types

If you have a preference for Sensing (S), you prefer to present facts and details in a step-by-step order. Intuitive types (N) may find it hard to attend to, or make sense of, facts unless you give them an outline or overview.

If you have a preference for Intuition (N), you prefer to provide an overview or outline of a topic first. Sensing types (S) may find it hard to attend to, or make sense of, an outline or overview unless you provide relevant facts and details.

Do You Provide Helpful Feedback to Others?

One of the most critical communication areas—and the one most fraught with difficulty—is giving feedback to others. People seek feedback, yet they often take feedback very personally. You need to determine the amount and type of feedback to give in different situations and learn to present it in a way that others are likely to accept.

Feedback given in a respectful way is a lot easier to listen to and acknowledge. People are more receptive to, and able to understand, feedback that consists of specific, concrete information and examples. Those who are unskilled at giving feedback tend to label or generalize rather than describe behaviors. The person who comes to work late can be labeled irresponsible or undependable. The person who has a conflict with a customer is grouchy or unfriendly. These labels are unhelpful. They can alienate or demean the person getting feedback, and they are a poor starting point for improving performance.

It's important to provide feedback as immediately as possible. Over time, our memories become distorted, and it's harder to describe and assess what happened. When you have feedback to offer, consider when the person will be most receptive to hearing it. Try to choose an optimal time and place for the communication. Keep privacy and confidentiality in mind.

When you give feedback, be direct. People may not accept or even recognize indirect feedback. Be open and honest, but avoid coming across as impersonal or blunt. This is another fine line. If you tend to be overly cautious or indirect, try to be more focused and to the point. If you tend to be overly direct, incorporate more consideration. Balance frankness and directness with compassion and caring.

Providing effective feedback

The checklist below offers tips for providing positive and corrective feedback. Check off the statements that reflect behaviors you already use. Review the statements you have not checked for ideas on how to improve this aspect of your communication.

When providing feedback, you should

- ☐ Offer positive comments and encouragement
- ☐ Discuss problem behaviors directly
- ☐ Avoid hinting or giving indirect feedback
- ☐ Be constructive and not destructive
- ☐ Choose an appropriate time and place
- ☐ Balance positive and corrective feedback
- ☐ Use clear, objective language
- ☐ Avoid making judgments, labeling, or blaming
- ☐ Describe specific behavior
- ☐ Provide concrete information and examples
- ☐ Deliver the feedback as soon as possible
- ☐ Assess when the hearer will be most receptive
- ☐ Balance frankness and directness with compassion and caring
- ☐ Avoid emotional remarks

> ## Excel Your Way:
> ## Tips for Thinking (T) and Feeling (F) types
>
> If you have a preference for Thinking (T), coworkers may misinterpret your direct, straightforward communications and language. When you mean to be direct and precise, others may see you as controlling or directing. Try softening your language.
>
> If you have a preference for Feeling (F), you may avoid speaking up about problematic behaviors. Others may assume nothing is wrong unless you state your perspective. Don't expect people to read your mind or anticipate your needs.

Corrective versus positive feedback

To perform effectively, people need a balance of positive and corrective feedback. Positive feedback allows people to see what they are doing well; it also can be highly motivating and encouraging. Many people thrive on appreciation. Corrective feedback is useful as well. People need to understand what they are not doing well and identify areas for improvement. Corrective feedback paves the way for problem solving and improved performance.

Purely positive feedback may make people feel good, but it won't help them develop. Purely corrective feedback can help people develop, but it doesn't add to morale or provide encouragement. No feedback at all, of course, is worst of all; without feedback, workers get neither encouragement nor information that will help them develop. Assess whether you offer sufficient feedback to others and whether you are more appreciative or analytic in your approach. Focus on providing both types of feedback.

Be sure your purpose for giving feedback is to help the recipient, the organization, or both. Don't give feedback simply to vent or to make yourself feel better. Consider the preferences of the person to whom you are providing feedback. Balance positive and corrective feedback to suit the person and the situation.

Excel Your Way: Tips for Thinking (T) and Feeling (F) types

If you have a preference for Thinking (T), positive feedback may seem an unnecessary exercise; you may think it simply states the obvious. Because you are highly self-evaluative and independent, you may not need or want someone to say what you already know you are doing right. However, you should recognize that others do seek this feedback. Challenge yourself to provide more positive feedback. Make sure you are sincere; others will know right away if your feedback is artificial.

If you have a preference for Feeling (F), providing corrective feedback may seem harsh and uncomfortable. You may avoid offering a critique because you want to prevent conflict or disharmony. However, you should recognize that people require this form of feedback to help them learn and grow. Challenge yourself to provide necessary corrective feedback. Make sure you are direct, as others may dismiss indirect comments.

Do You Deal Effectively with Conflict?

Many work relationships involve differences of opinion. When conflicts arise, several ineffective habits can keep you from solving issues and working cooperatively. Some people avoid or ignore issues or complain to others rather than approaching conflicts directly. Some people are unwilling to see situations from other perspectives and approach conflicts with solutions that are only acceptable to some of the people involved. Others have difficulty letting go of past conflicts. These ineffective habits lead to frustration and further conflict, and they negatively affect the atmosphere and morale of the workplace.

To build a successful career, you must identify and resolve interpersonal issues. Listening carefully and expressing yourself clearly are good starting points for resolving conflicts. Following a set of conflict-resolution steps also can help you resolve difficulties.

This part of the chapter describes a positive model for approaching conflict based on mutual respect.

Resolving issues

Use the list below to check off the effective conflict-resolution behaviors you already use. Practice all of these behaviors.

Positive conflict-resolution behaviors

- ☐ Addressing the conflict
- ☐ Speaking directly to others who are involved in the conflict
- ☐ Remaining calm and reasonable
- ☐ Engaging positively in a conflict-resolution process
- ☐ Listening openly to others' perspectives
- ☐ Looking for a solution that benefits everyone
- ☐ Letting issues go when they are resolved

The following section outlines concrete steps for dealing with conflicts. Throughout the conflict-resolution process, listen carefully and express your point of view clearly. Avoid becoming personally engaged in the process; assess your biases and strive to be objective.

It takes two to solve a problem. If the individual or group of people with whom you are conflicting are not interested in solving a problem, your hands are tied. In this situation, all you can do is control your reactions and remain open to the possibility that others may step up to work with you. Here are some questions that will help you determine whether all parties are interested in, and willing to put energy toward, solving the problem.

Is everyone ready for conflict resolution?

- Can everyone see and validate alternative perspectives and needs?
- Are they all willing to negotiate and compromise?
- Will they all treat others with respect and equality?
- Do they consider others' needs as important as their own?
- Is everyone objective and calm?

- Is everyone focused on the problem, not the person?
- Is everyone focused on a positive outcome for all parties?

If everyone does not have the right mindset, conflict resolution may not be successful. In these cases, you need to decide whether the issue is important enough to pursue. Sometimes it is best to avoid, or find a way to work around, people who are unreceptive to dealing with issues. However, this is not a good strategy if the conflict is significantly affecting you or your work. You may need to show the other person or people involved the importance of finding a win-win solution. When both parties are willing, you can take steps to resolve the conflict.

If this is not possible, you may need to find a third party to help work out your differences. Try to deal with coworker conflicts directly before going to a supervisor. If your efforts fail, explain to the coworker that you plan to talk to the supervisor. Don't make this a threat; simply explain, clearly and calmly, that the issue needs to be resolved so you can work effectively.

Sometimes extremely thorny problems or lack of trust or rapport make it very difficult to solve interpersonal issues without external assistance. Use your judgment to assess the situation, and then get some assistance if necessary. However, in many cases you can use the steps below to work through issues with others.

Conflict Resolution Steps

Here is a four-step conflict-resolution process you can use to deal with interpersonal issues.

Step 1: Identify the needs of each individual involved.

Be sure everyone expresses his or her needs, wants, and fears. Use effective listening and information sharing to focus on understanding and appreciating everyone's perspective. The broader the perspective of each member in the conflict, the likelier you are to find a resolution that satisfies everyone. This is not a time for judging or arguing about perspectives. Your focus should be on listening to understand.

Attack the problem, not the people involved. Avoid expressing your needs in terms of solutions. This limits the process of generating creative, win-win outcomes. For example, consider the effect of saying, "I need the boardroom every Thursday." This statement includes an implicit solution: the only way to fill the need is to hand over the boardroom every Thursday. Now consider the effect of saying, "I need a space to meet with a group of six people, preferably in the morning on Thursdays." This statement addresses the purpose rather than the solution; because it addresses the need in an open-ended way, it can result in a variety of win-win solutions.

Think "outside the box." Strive to define the problem as clearly as possible. Separate needs from wants. At the same time, focus on your fears and emotions. In the example above, you may have feared embarrassing yourself and losing a customer if you went to the boardroom for a scheduled meeting and found it already occupied. Perhaps you were also concerned that the customer might see you as incompetent or inefficient. Also, seek to understand the other person's fears, emotions, and needs. By the end of this first step, everyone's needs should be heard, understood, and validated. If this does not occur, you are not likely to come to a satisfactory solution.

Step 2: Take a win-win approach to generating possible solutions.

When people's needs are on the table, think of creative options that will address everyone's concerns. See the situation as an opportunity that will have positive outcomes. Share power and respect everyone as an equal in the process. Taking a win-win approach may require you to shift from a competitive to a collaborative framework.

People with a competitive mindset see conflict situations as win-or-lose fights over limited resources. When someone has this mindset, conflicts can turn into power struggles. People who have a collaborative mindset assume that situations have unlimited possibilities and options. Instead of competing for a specific boardroom, for example, collaborative thinkers maximize and capitalize on all possible meeting spaces within the organization to meet everyone's needs.

This collaborative approach differs markedly from the highly individualistic focus common in North American business culture. You may need to challenge your thinking to operate within a win-win framework. For effective conflict resolution, all parties must want everyone to benefit. Mutual gain is the expected outcome. When this is established, everyone can brainstorm and explore options. Be willing to accommodate and show flexibility. See yourself as a partner rather than a competitor as you move through this process. If there is a significant difference in positional power between two parties in conflict, it is especially important to address respect and equality issues.

Step 3: Reach agreement on a solution.

After exploring options, the parties need to choose a solution that provides the best outcome for everyone involved. This may involve some negotiation. People may want to explore which tradeoffs and compromises might be acceptable. Everyone can then evaluate proposed solutions based on how well they meet everyone's needs. To avoid misunderstandings, be sure everyone agrees with the solution you choose.

Step 4: Move together toward a solution.

After you decide on a solution, make sure you follow through. Depending on the circumstances, it might help to write out a plan or agreement. Even if the agreement remains verbal, confirm that the steps and desired outcomes of the plan are clear to everyone.

Relating to Anyone: Personality Type Strengths and Challenges

All personality types can relate to anyone. Every personality type has unique strengths and challenges aligned to their natural preferences. Read through the information on your personality type for suggestions specifically tailored to your natural way of working.

Responders (ESTP and ESFP)

Responders prefer short, to-the-point communications. You send clear, useful messages that focus on facts and realities. Others may want you to add more structure or background information to your communications and link information about the situation at hand to other ideas or future considerations. Your preference for Thinking (ESTP) or Feeling (ESFP) influences your tendency for providing more positive or corrective feedback. However, in both cases, your feedback is likely practical and immediate. Your focus on the tasks at hand may get in the way of dealing with long-term or complex conflicts or issues. You may need to develop patience for finding and working through underlying patterns or causes of conflict. As long as others know you are serious about dealing with issues, your playful and flexible approach will help you defuse some of the tension in conflict.

Explorers (ENTP and ENFP)

Explorers tend to communicate with enthusiasm and energy. You may, at times, seem *overly* enthusiastic. Because you focus on ideas and the future, your communications may be too abstract, disorganized, and vague. Practice being sequential, organized, and detailed. Cue others when you are changing topics; explain the "leaps" in your thinking so they can follow your train of thought. Your preference for Thinking (ENTP) or Feeling (ENFP) influences your tendency for providing more positive or corrective feedback. However, in both cases, your feedback is likely targeted toward helping others make global or long-term changes. In conflict you may find it easy to see alternative points of view, but you may not always take the time to listen carefully. Your interest in generating ideas can help you pinpoint win-win possibilities for dealing with issues. Just remember to follow up on your course of action.

Expeditors (ESTJ and ENTJ)

Expeditors tend to take a direct and concise approach to communications, focusing on competencies, goals, actions, and results. Because you are very comfortable critiquing, debating and competing, you may be surprised to learn that others interpret these behaviors negatively. Accommodate others when you communicate by choosing your words carefully; avoid coming across as overly directive or abrupt. Provide positive as well as corrective feedback. You are always interested in accomplishing tasks and moving forward; you may need to develop patience for exploring others' perspectives and considering a range of win-win options for solving conflicts. Otherwise coworkers may feel you aren't listening to them, and they may resist coming to closure until you acknowledge their views. As long as you don't choose and argue for a solution too early in the process, your interest in solving problems and implementing solutions will move the conflict-resolution process forward.

Contributors (ESFJ and ENFJ)

Contributors are interested in understanding people's values, opinions, and reactions. You tend to communicate in a warm, friendly, empathic, and appreciative manner. In a work environment, others may feel that your emphasis on personal communications distracts them from getting to the tasks at hand. Limit small talk in these situations. You are usually quick to offer positive feedback, but you may find it difficult to provide corrective feedback because you don't want to disrupt group harmony. Strive to provide both positive and corrective feedback to others as appropriate. You find it hard to ignore differences of opinion linked to personal relationships and values. When coworkers feel unappreciated or undervalued, you may have a tendency to overwork issues. Attempting to resolve everyone's issues at work will overwhelm and exhaust you. Set some boundaries and carefully choose which issues to work through. Your focus on collaboration, cooperation, and inclusion is very useful when you choose to resolve important conflicts.

Assimilators (ISTJ and ISFJ)

When communicating, Assimilators tend to be comprehensive, accurate, and precise, focusing on facts and real-life examples. While you prefer to process information internally before discussing a topic or taking action, others may wish you would present your opinions more frequently. You can't always take as much time as you'd like to think things over. On-the-spot interactions may be stressful for you, but learning to speak up without delay cues people to your interest and engagement. You prefer to understand topics in depth, and when you choose to share information, you sometimes give too much detail. Not everyone wants to know about a topic thoroughly. Summarize and generalize so you can explain information concisely. Your preference for Thinking (ISTJ) or Feeling (ISFJ) influences your tendency to provide more positive or corrective feedback. However, in both cases, your feedback is likely targeted toward finding practical solutions. During conflict resolution, ask for time to plan your communications before you discuss the issue.

Visionaries (INTJ and INFJ)

Visionaries are big-picture thinkers who focus on communicating complex concepts and theories rather than facts and details. Your preference for communicating using models, metaphors, and analogies may make it hard for you to explain your ideas simply. Challenge yourself to offer straightforward explanations that describe practical realities, facts, and details in a step-by-step manner. Minimize your use of symbolic language and figures of speech. One of your greatest communication challenges is to share ideas before they become too entrenched in your mind. When you have processed an idea thoroughly, you may have trouble accepting new input. At the same time, you may be uncomfortable sharing an idea until you have thought it through. Find balance so you do not appear resistant to new input. Your preference for Thinking (INTJ) or Feeling (INFJ) influences your tendency to provide more positive or corrective feedback. However, in both cases, you likely target your feedback toward long-term changes. Your ability to see future implications and consequences of decisions helps you resolve conflicts.

Analyzers (ISTP and INTP)

Analyzers tend to be direct, frank, and concise. You usually do not take things personally, except perhaps when your competence is being challenged. You usually deal with almost any situation calmly and objectively. You may not see a logical reason for small talk, developing rapport, or sharing feelings at work and therefore may find these activities unappealing. You may use sarcasm or be cynical or critical in your communications, and you tend to enjoy arguments, debates, and challenges. Although these forms of interaction seem logical to you, others may misinterpret them as indifference or detachment. You are not likely to provide positive feedback to others; in particular, generalized statements such as "good job," which state the obvious, strike you as useless. Although you mean no harm, other types may respond negatively to your interaction style. Depending on their preferences, they may seek positive feedback and opportunities to build rapport, and they may dislike debates. When you communicate with coworkers, consider personal and situational factors; don't simply analyze and critique. Accommodating others will result in more effective interactions and efficient conflict resolution.

Enhancers (ISFP and INFP)

Enhancers prefer to communicate in a comfortable, low-key, one-on-one setting and tend to be supportive, empathic, quiet, and sensitive. Others see you as accommodating and nurturing. You may react personally to what is being said, and you may struggle to be objective, especially in situations that involve conflict or challenge. In these cases you may stop accommodating others and become withdrawn and stubborn, especially if your core personal values are challenged. Although you are usually committed to maintaining harmony and avoiding conflict, in the long term you may benefit from asserting your opinions and feelings. Carefully monitor your reactions when you receive corrective feedback; try to avoid feeling personally attacked. Challenge yourself to offer corrective feedback to help others learn and grow. Engage in conflict resolution even if it makes you uncomfortable. Use your ability to understand others' situations to help you brainstorm win-win options.

Reflection and Action

This chapter shows why relating to anyone is essential. When people communicate successfully, they work collaboratively and build important networks to facilitate their career success. You can improve your ability to relate to anyone by planning your communications, offering positive and corrective feedback and resolving conflicts. Do you relate well to anyone? Look at your responses to the checklists in the chapter and think about the suggestions offered. In the area below, write out some steps you can take to improve your ability to relate to others.

CHAPTER SEVEN

Cultivate Your Curiosity

People on the road to career success are eager to learn new things. They seek new information that will help them do their work more effectively. When you cultivate your curiosity, you find and study new information and then apply it to your work. You manage large amounts of information by logically analyzing, critiquing, and summarizing. You integrate and link new information to what you already know and understand. As a result, you are a lifelong learner. When you cultivate your curiosity, others see you as interested, up-to-date, knowledgeable, and aware. They are confident in your ability to easily learn new skills and apply new information. They keep you in mind when new opportunities or challenges arise.

People who don't cultivate their curiosity rely on prior learning. They don't ask questions or seek new information. They accept the information they are given at face value, without checking or critiquing it. Their knowledge is often outdated and inaccurate, and they tend to stay out of discussions about new ideas or information. People who lack curiosity may use technology ineptly or unwillingly. Others don't seek them out as a source of information. They may be passed over for new or interesting projects because others are unsure of their ability to learn the relevant information or develop the necessary skills.

The following checklist can help you determine how well you are cultivating your curiosity. Each of these behaviors shows curiosity at work. If you don't check off a statement, look for ways to increase that behavior.

Ways to cultivate your curiosity

- ☐ Using resources (such as dictionaries, manuals) in the workplace
- ☐ Asking questions or seeking new information from others
- ☐ Subscribing to and reading appropriate periodicals or updates
- ☐ Effectively using Internet search engines
- ☐ Honing computer and technical literacy
- ☐ Using new information when completing work tasks
- ☐ Discussing new ideas or information
- ☐ Acting as an information source for others

Can You Find What You Need to Know?

Curious workers actively seek and use new information. To keep current, you must constantly seek out new information. This learning will translate into better performance at work.

Take an active role in your learning by determining what and where you want to learn and by choosing the best sources of information. A curious mind asks questions to figure out what and how to learn. As you sift through information, ask questions to hone your search for knowledge. Here are some questions to help you focus your search for information.

Targeting your learning

- What do I need (or want) to know?
- Where can I find the information?
- Would I understand the information better if it were in a different form?
- Is the information relevant to my work?
- How can I use the information?
- Can others benefit from the information?
- Should I remember or store the information?

Where can I find what I need to know?

Curious workers use multiple sources of information to help them learn and develop. Use the list of information sources below as a starting point for thinking about what you will learn next. If you can demonstrate that these resources will help you become more productive, your employer may be willing to pay for some of them.

- *The Internet*: The Internet has a wealth of information on a wide range of topics. Completing targeted searches on specific topics or even surfing for general information can provide lots of new facts and ideas.
- *Libraries*: Your public library is a vast and economical information source. You can find all sorts of information at your local branch, and you can order resources from other libraries. Libraries provide great learning alternatives such as books, magazines, newspapers, videos, CDs, and DVDs.
- *Association memberships*: When you join an association, you receive newsletters, updates, website access, and information about new developments and upcoming learning events. Associations also provide information and resources to help you obtain credentials and certification.
- *Periodical publications*: Many professions have journals or magazines that summarize key knowledge and highlight new trends or developments. Even the advertisements can point out trends in your field. If you join an association, you usually get journals or newsletters with the membership.
- *Conferences and trade shows*: Many industries sponsor trade shows and conferences that highlight current and new practices. These events also provide opportunities to network and meet people who can help advance your career.
- *Courses and workshops*: These more formal learning opportunities can provide you with credentials and credits as well as information and networking opportunities.
- *Radio, movies, CDs, DVDs, and television*: Electronic media offer a variety of educational resources that may provide both general knowledge and specialized information.
- *People*: You can learn from everyone. Coworkers, customers, supervisors, leaders, friends, and family may all have something to offer. Ask questions and listen to others. Mentors, especially those with expertise in the work you want to do, can greatly facilitate your career success. Social networking websites can provide broad access to groups, experts, and information.

Those who shy away from new technology are at a great disadvantage when it comes to accessing information and achieving career success. Younger workers may have learned how to make connections and search for information, especially on the Internet, through school assignments and life experiences; others may learn to use new technology on the job. Assess your skill level and comfort with current technology, and look into courses at public libraries and colleges if you need to hone your skills.

Excel Your Way: Tips for Extraverts (E) and Introverts (I)

If you have a preference for Extraversion (E), you may choose breadth over depth when exploring a topic. You may want to discuss or apply new information before taking time to read, listen, and reflect on details, and you are drawn to resources that you can use quickly. You also prefer learning opportunities that offer occasions to interact with others.

If you have a preference for Introversion (I), you may want to understand topics in depth. You seek opportunities to read, listen, and reflect before discussing and applying information. Complete and comprehensive resources are attractive to you, as are learning opportunities that provide time and space to reflect on new information.

Avoid information overload

You may be intimidated or overwhelmed by the sheer volume of information available today, and as a result you may avoid or ignore information. Taking in new information is time consuming; you not only need to find and understand information, but you also need to decide whether to memorize it, use it, store it, remember where to find it, or discard it. Information is biased and can be unhelpful or incomplete. To simplify your information-gathering process, use the critiquing skills in this chapter. Scan information to sort out what is accurate and relevant. Then decide what you need to do with the information.

In our rapidly changing work world, it is sometimes more important to find information than to memorize and retain the information. You do not need to learn and remember everything. Finding information effectively can be as useful as remembering it in many situations. However, in other situations you may need data at your fingertips. Identify and separate what you must know and recall immediately from what you can access, as needed, from external sources. When you need to apply a number of key pieces of information, don't expect yourself to recall it accurately and completely; simply keep it in an easily accessible place. For example, keep information sheets, procedure manuals, and other written or visual cues close at hand to serve as memory aids. Create a system for summarizing, storing, and finding information you don't need to remember.

E-mail has exploded as an information-sharing tool, especially in large organizations. This instant communication channel has advantages and disadvantages. Many people receive a large volume of e-mail on a regular basis, and it can easily become overwhelming. Develop a concrete strategy to deal with, store, or delete e-mail messages. Manage your electronic inbox the same way you manage paperwork. Get rid of messages you don't need and create files for information you need to keep. Learn to scan messages and set aside specific times for managing e-mail.

The Internet can be overwhelming too. When you look for information online, try out various search engines and databases. Limit your searches to produce less numerous and more relevant information links. As mentioned earlier, many schools and libraries offer courses that can help you sharpen your computer skills and Internet savvy.

Excel Your Way: Tips for Judging (J) and Perceiving (P) types

If you have a preference for Judging (J), you may be tempted to find the information you need from a credible source and move on to a new topic. This is an efficient strategy, but at times you may stop your research too early and miss important alternative or conflicting information and perspectives.

If you have a preference for Perceiving (P), you can easily become distracted while searching the Internet. One site may lead to another, more interesting one. Recognize when you are becoming distracted by tangential topics or ideas and refocus on the topic you are researching,

Are You Well Informed?

Not all information is created equal. Taking information at face value is a dangerous practice. Develop strategies to determine how valuable and accurate information is. Critique and evaluate information sources for biases and credibility. Find multiple sources to confirm information and separate facts from opinions. The following questions can help you analyze and evaluate information sources.

Where does the information come from?

- Who collected the information? Why?
- Who wrote about the information? What do they know about the topic? Are they biased?
- What is the author's point of view?
- Who published the information? What biases or assumptions might they have?
- Why was the information published? Who was it published for?

What kind of information is it?

- How old is the information?
- Is the information opinion or fact?
- Do the authors use emotionally loaded words?
- Is this promotional material? (Are the authors trying to sell a product, service, concept, or candidate?)
- Who was included in the data? Who was not?
- If it is research, does the researcher use a sample that accurately represents the group?

Is the information credible?

- Can the conclusions be drawn logically from the evidence at hand?
- What assumptions are being made?
- If relationships are being shown, are they cause and effect?
- Do facts or research support the main idea?
- Is there any reason to question the information?
- What conclusions or evaluations can you make about the information?

Is the information useful?

- How does this information compare with other information on the topic?
- What information is not included?
- How might this information be relevant to you?
- Who might be able to use this information?
- What are your own biases on this topic? How do they affect what you believe?

What other information might be useful?

- Where might you get information on the same topic with a different bias or perspective? (There is no unbiased information, only information with different biases.)
- Do you need more information on this topic?
- How can you get more information?

In this age of readily available information, it is extremely important to evaluate information sources critically. Find out when the information was collected. Outdated information is often worse than no information at all. This is especially true if the information is related to procedures, regulations, or other requirements. Watch out for older print resources that have not been updated or revised. Information can change quickly, and out-of-date resources are, at best, inaccurate and misleading. The Internet often offers more recent information, but bear in mind that the dates and sources of Internet information also need to be checked.

Checking for credibility

Evaluate the credibility of any information source. Do this by checking out the credentials of the authors, identifying biases or affiliations, and researching sources' backgrounds. When assessing data, you need to find out who collected it and why. Determine the purpose of the information and the author's point of view. This will help you identify bias.

Accessing multiple sources can help you further evaluate information, but multiple sources may also provide confusing or contradictory data. Sorting out the contexts, sources, and biases in the different perspectives can be a daunting task. Various credible sources may focus on unique aspects of a topic and thus provide different conclusions. Identify the assumptions underlying the reasoning in the arguments. Also be alert to your own assumptions and biases, and be open-minded when gathering information.

Separating fact from fiction

You also need to separate opinion from fact and speculation from research. You must analyze facts and research to determine whether the context and findings are applicable to your work situation. Facts can be proved. Predictions, guesses, and opinions are individual reactions to a topic. Keep these information sources separate, and consider their nature when you draw a conclusion. When evaluating information, identify authors' underlying assumptions. Recognize and evaluate the kinds of evidence they use to support an argument or position.

Facts and opinions are both helpful sources of information. Be aware that when information is used to persuade others, only certain facts are included. Opinions may initially seem less reliable, but they can also provide valuable information. Just keep the experts' biases in mind.

Drawing conclusions

See what conclusions you can draw from the evidence at hand. Explore and determine whether the evidence indicates a cause-and-effect relationship. Events may occur together without being causally related. Bear in mind that events have both direct and indirect causes—and most events have multiple causes. You need to understand these relationships when you analyze information. People can jump to a conclusion when they are influenced by erroneous arguments. Don't let this happen to you. Carefully consider all of the facts at hand.

Facts are especially difficult to sort out when information sources are biased toward marketing or promoting something. Promotional materials often are misleading. Testimonials, guarantees, promises, and other sales strategies are designed to promote rather than inform. Recognize and critique these persuasive strategies for what they are. If you make purchases and recommend vendors and services, build your awareness of sales and marketing techniques. You may find it helpful to create a checklist or set of criteria for evaluating purchasing options; it can help you clarify your needs and think about purchases analytically.

Success Story: Too Good to Be True

A young woman with ENFP personality type preferences was looking for educational options to pursue a career teaching drama. She found an Internet site describing a wonderful program in an idyllic setting. She enthusiastically pursued the opportunity to attend the school. Her career counselor encouraged her to find out more before applying. On closer inspection, the woman learned that the program was extremely expensive and the credential it offered was not accepted by her local educational system. Although still optimistic about opportunities, she has learned to complete more research before becoming excited about programs described in advertisements and promotional materials.

Look for biases

People can be emotional or biased when evaluating information. We are much likelier to accept and remember information consonant with our belief system, and we tend to reject or ignore information that does not align with our beliefs. Explore your own biases and consider what kinds of information you are likely to discard or believe.

Excel Your Way: Tips for Thinking (T) and Feeling (F) types

If you have a preference for Thinking (T), you naturally spot flaws and evaluate what you see and hear. You are drawn to analysis and evaluation, so you are more easily convinced by logic than by personal opinions. Strive to avoid automatically dismissing personal opinions.

If you have a preference for Feeling (F), you naturally appreciate rather than analyze. You are more easily convinced by an argument that aligns to your personal values or beliefs than by logic. You may need to step outside your natural preferences to logically evaluate information.

Do You Know How to Learn?

Think about how you prefer to learn. Some people are visual learners. They learn best when they see what they are learning. Videos, diagrams, illustrations, and other visual learning aids facilitate their learning. Others are auditory learners and learn best when they hear or discuss information. Still others prefer hands-on learning and are most successful when they try tasks and work directly with materials. When you choose learning opportunities, try to incorporate all three modes: seeing, hearing, and doing. At the end of this chapter, you'll find additional learning strengths and preferences related to your personality type; these can help you further customize your learning strategies.

No matter what your preferences, you must take in, remember or store, and then use information. If you don't complete this information-processing loop, you risk losing or distorting what you learned. Assess your learning needs, weaknesses, and strengths in the information-processing loop. For example, you may have difficulty paying attention, recalling a sequence, understanding verbal directions, interpreting visual information, or memorizing facts. Everyone can improve their information processing. A corporate executive may be articulate, brilliant, and innovative, yet he or she may need to carry a pocket spellchecker.

To quickly assess your potential learning difficulties, analyze the types of errors you make when you learn new material or complete work tasks. Many people under-utilize error analysis, but it is a powerful learning tool. Thinking about errors and mistakes in this way helps you identify practical ways to correct your behavior. Problems always have many possible causes—and many potential solutions. For example, if you have trouble remembering sequences, you can learn to summarize and write down the steps in the sequence. If you struggle to remember what you hear, you can take notes. If you tend to forget names in a meeting, you can make a diagram of the table and jot down people's names as they are introduced; if you are presenting to the group, you can hand out nametags. Come up with practical and specific ways to get around your difficulties.

Making mistakes is an essential part of learning. If you look carefully at the types and patterns of mistakes you make, you can learn from them and do your work with fewer errors. The key to learning from mistakes is taking responsibility and analyzing what happened. When you figure out why the error is happening, take action to fix it. Whenever possible, create a long-term solution to avoid future errors. See Chapter 4 for more information about taking responsibility and learning from mistakes.

> ## *Success Story: What Did You Learn?*
>
> A young man walked into the Department of Motor Vehicles and took an exam to obtain his learner's permit. He failed the exam. The examiner asked if he would like to see his results. The young man said no and walked away. He complained to a friend on the way out that he had now failed the exam three times. This young man was given the chance to learn from his mistakes and dismissed it. Had he made an effort to understand what he didn't know, he could have studied those areas in preparation for his next exam. Another young man, watching this transaction, vowed to take advantage of the offer for feedback if he did not pass his test.

Be an efficient reader

Reading is an especially important way to take in information. Before you start to read, you should identify what you want to accomplish through your reading. You read a description of detailed operating procedures with one set of goals in mind; you read a global statement of business objectives with another. Reading a training manual may involve formal learning and memorization; reading an operating manual may involve familiarizing yourself with the table of contents. E-mail that describes an organizational change may simply require you to edit some phone numbers and contact information. In order to read effectively, keep the purpose of reading in mind.

Think about what you are reading

Ask yourself questions to determine how to approach a reading task. Scan the material to get an overview of the content. Think about how you might organize and use the information. Define a purpose for your reading and decide to what depth you need to read. For example, you may not have time to carefully study an extensive manual, but you may find it helpful to look at key sections.

Questions to ask yourself before you start your reading

- Does the reading material include one or more features (overviews, objectives, and so on) that summarize what is important?

- Are there any learning aids such as a table of contents, headings, charts, graphs, diagrams, illustrations, worksheets, italicized words, glossaries, appendices, indexes, bibliography, underlining, or summaries?
- What content does the material cover?
- Why do I need to read this? What do I want to get out of the reading?
- Is it necessary to read all of the material or only certain parts?
- Does the material have familiar terminology and vocabulary or should I keep a dictionary close by?
- Are there related materials that will make this reading clearer or more complete?

Questions to keep your mind active when reading

- What is the main idea here?
- Is this an example, illustration, or supporting detail?
- How much detail do I need to know?
- Should I take notes?
- Do I already know this information?
- Do I need to remember this?
- Does this relate to anything I already know? How is it the same? How is it different?

Make a summary

Summarize main points and important details. Some people find that taking notes adds sensory input to learning and helps them pay attention and remember the content. By summarizing you also can avoid rereading extensively. Summaries can be a major time saver, especially when you will be tested on your learning. Note taking is most effective when you focus on what is important and use your own words.

You can summarize reading materials in several ways. Some people like to write summary notes in the margins of the material or write a summary on a separate page. Others prefer to use a highlighter or underline important points. Using a variety of colored highlighter pens can cue you to different aspects of the material. Highlight only 10 to 20 percent of the material. Index cards with questions or cues on one side and information on the other can be especially helpful for learning terminology. If keeping the cards organized is a problem, punch holes in them and put them on a binder ring.

You can take notes by writing questions on one side of the page and information on the other. You can organize appropriate types of information into tables, graphs, pictures, flow charts, illustrations, maps, or outlines. You can use computer programs designed to create these different kinds of information organizers. Classifying and categorizing information is another helpful way to summarize, as is linking or charting relationships within the information. You can apply these same processes to information that is provided verbally in meetings, seminars, training, workshops, and courses.

Excel Your Way:
Tips for Sensing (S) and Intuitive (N) types

If you have a preference for Sensing (S), you may find it easier to summarize information by starting with the facts and details. From this practical starting point, you can build a framework to organize tangible information step-by-step. You may find outlines, charts, tables, and highlighting useful.

If you have a preference for Intuition (N), you first see connections and links. Create a broad framework for the information you are learning, and then attend to and organize the details by integrating them into your framework. Your summary likely will be global and random rather than structured and orderly. You may find overviews, models, metaphors, mind mapping, and flow charts helpful.

Although it is important to summarize, it is just as important to avoid overgeneralizing based on a small number of examples. Summarizing information too broadly can mask important details. Carefully consider the depth and breadth of information you need to absorb. If the details are more than you can store in your memory, create an information storage system to help you find the required information quickly and effectively. A pocket-size booklet containing key information can be a valuable job aid.

Success Story: Referring, Not Remembering

Here is a strategy one worker used to recall a frequently used sequence. A man with INFJ personality type preferences had considerable difficulty recalling the correct sequence of steps for translating a document from one software form to another. Rather than tax his sequential memory, he simply created a sheet that summarized the required steps. He photocopied the steps onto a heavy sheet of paper and stored the job aid near the computer. His problem was solved.

Review material

After about 15 to 20 minutes of reading, stop and consider how much information has stuck. This will help ensure that you are paying attention and retaining information while reading. If you read the words on a page without putting in the effort to understand or remember the information, you won't learn anything.

Studies of learning effectiveness indicate that people remember best when they study material repeatedly and review what they read within 24 hours of first reading it. Short, frequent review sessions are most effective. To retain as much information as possible, don't simply read and reread; test yourself on what you've learned. You can ask yourself questions based on your notes, write down what you remember from your reading, or have someone ask you questions.

Reading difficult materials

Some learning materials are particularly challenging. They may require a high level of reading comprehension and use unfamiliar language and vocabulary. Many topics have their own terms, or jargon. Acronyms and technical terminology can be very confusing at first. Some companies use so many acronyms that they list them in the orientation package they hand out to new workers.

Here are some strategies for dealing with jargon or other unfamiliar vocabulary.

- Use a glossary or index if one is provided.
- Learn a new word every day. Study it. Find a way to use it.
- Keep a dictionary close at hand (or bookmarked online) and use it often.
- Invest in a pocket dictionary.
- Write down definitions. Include examples, illustrations, and applications.
- Use your own words to define unfamiliar terms.

Watch for signs of eyestrain or eye problems. If you experience persistent symptoms such as reading-related headaches, difficulty seeing print clearly, or red or sore eyes, make an appointment with an optometrist.

If you have trouble comprehending what you read and suspect you have learning difficulties, speak to a psychologist who specializes in learning. A learning specialist can assess areas of difficulty and suggest concrete, work-related accommodations.

Integrate and apply what you learn

Cultivating your curiosity is not just a matter of learning and applying new information directly; you also need to transfer what you learn to new situations. For example, if a customer-service course teaches a strategy for developing empathy and rapport with a customer, students ideally will link the information they learn in this context to a variety of other situations, such as interacting with colleagues or leaders.

When learning, think about your past experiences and make links between what you are learning now and previous situations. For example, suppose a student in the customer-service class finds it difficult to listen without making judgments or offering solutions. This experience may stimulate a number of associations for the student if he or she thinks about strategies and success in the bigger picture. Perhaps a supervisor previously gave feedback about the student's overly directive leadership approach, or the student's teenage child complained that the parent was judging rather than listening. By making links to other situations, the learner can transfer his or her learning.

Transfer of learning only occurs when you relate learning to other situations and experiences. Here are some examples of questions to help you link, integrate, and transfer new information.

- Do I know something about the topic already?
- How does what I am learning now relate to what I already know?

- Does the information relate to other situations?
- How can I use the information in other situations?
- Does the information fit with what I already know?
- If the information doesn't fit with what I know, what specifically doesn't fit?

Cultivating Your Curiosity: Personality Type Strengths and Challenges

All personality types can cultivate their curiosity. Every personality type has unique strengths and challenges aligned to their natural preferences. Read through the information on your personality type for suggestions specifically tailored to your natural way of working.

Responders (ESTP and ESFP)

Responders are interested in learning information that is fun, practical, and immediately useful. You prefer hands-on or active learning to sitting and reading or listening. When learning, find ways to interact with the learning materials and to use what you are learning immediately. When possible, negotiate more active options for assignments; for example, see if you can apply learning to the workplace instead of writing a theoretical paper. If you need to study for extended periods, break your learning into short, specific, quickly attainable segments, and reward yourself with a break between each segment. Highlight relevant facts and interesting data when you read highly detailed materials; take notes when you listen. When you need to learn abstract information, find concrete links between theory, facts, and applications. This will make the information more real and useful. To maintain your attention when reading, minimize distractions in your immediate environment. Keep yourself focused by changing activities. Schedule time just before deadlines to accommodate your "just in time" style. Start larger learning projects, such as papers or reports, early to avoid last-minute stress.

Explorers (ENTP and ENFP)

Explorers enjoy learning about new ideas and new ways of doing things. You look for opportunities to link theories and models in a broad, general way. When you are learning a new topic, find a model or framework that can help you integrate and conceptually organize the material. Use a model that easily incorporates multiple sources of information. Because you want to discuss information to build on ideas, you may find it difficult to learn in highly structured, lecture-based learning settings. In these situations, try writing out your thoughts and questions during class. Then discuss the information with other interested learners. This process will build depth into your learning and will help you cope with situations in which you are not encouraged to comment or contribute. Seek learning environments that do invite discussion. When you research or write about a topic, set a time to stop exploring and start producing a product. Otherwise you may find yourself distracted by many tangential topics and ideas. Schedule time just before deadlines to accommodate your "just in time" style. Start larger learning projects, such as papers or reports, early to avoid last-minute stress.

Expeditors (ESTJ and ENTJ)

Expeditors are interested in finding expedient ways to reach learning goals and objectives. You want to develop competencies that will help you accomplish your work more efficiently. Ensure that your learning environment is organized and structured for results. Find learning opportunities led by a highly competent teacher with subject-area expertise. You like to learn as independently as possible. Avoid highly regimented or directive learning situations. Seek out credible and objective learning resources. Define your learning outcomes and learn with others who are achievement oriented, curious, and focused. Open-ended discussions may strike you as inefficient learning tools, but try to develop the patience to listen to and learn from alternative points of view. When you are involved in collaborative learning projects, take time to learn about the people in your group; it will lead to a more effective group process. Learn by questioning, critiquing, and evaluating subject matter, but be careful not to offend or overwhelm your fellow learners or your instructor with your assertive learning style.

Contributors (ESFJ and ENFJ)

Contributors are interested in learning new information that has a positive effect on people's lives. You prefer to learn in a structured, well-organized, supportive environment that provides positive feedback and encouragement. In disorganized or more open-ended learning settings, create your own order to facilitate your learning. Seek out learning environments that offer collaborative and interactive approaches. Find instructors who take time to develop group rapport and emphasize group dynamics. If you do not have a supportive learning environment, find co-learners who are interested in working cooperatively outside the learning setting. You want to ensure that everyone is included in the learning process, and you enjoy learning from the experience and expertise of other learners. But be careful not to allow other learners' needs to interfere with your own learning process. Learning usually involves corrective feedback. Ideally you will receive gentle, sensitive feedback, but at times you need to learn from frank, objective comments. See it as a valuable learning tool rather than an affront.

Assimilators (ISTJ and ISFJ)

Assimilators want to learn information that is relevant to their experiences. When learning, you build up a rich experiential base to which you constantly add new facts and details. You take time to examine new information carefully and determine how it fits with what you know from experience. To facilitate your learning, focus on practical, in-depth, accurate, useful information and take time alone to fully assimilate what you learn. If you are taking a class, read learning materials before class whenever possible. Because you prefer structure and predictability, find out as much as possible about exam formats or assignment expectations and marking criteria. Study by reproducing the conditions of the exam as closely as possible. (For example, study for an essay exam by writing out essays.) Organize information in a clear, structured manner by making step-by-step procedures, creating charts, categorizing facts, and completing checklists. When learning theoretical information, link the ideas to facts you know about the topic. When answering broad, abstract questions, begin by writing down facts and details. Then organize and relate the relevant facts to the given question.

Visionaries (INTJ and INFJ)

Visionaries want to learn about complex ideas and are drawn to theories and models. You prefer learning settings that provide varied resources and introduce alternative models and multiple perspectives. When you are exposed to new ideas, you like to have time alone to process, integrate, and evaluate the information. Precise language and conceptual clarity are important to you, so seek instructors who know the topic well and who are conversant in alternative explanations and perspectives. You are easily bored by routine or simple, straightforward learning exercises, so you seek and may negotiate fewer, but more complex, learning projects and assignments. Learning independently appeals to Visionaries. When you research and write about new ideas, restrict your exploration. Narrowing the scope of the topic will enable you to move toward closure and apply the information. You may not naturally enjoy learning facts and details. Try thinking of them as examples of, or exceptions to, concepts. After organizing the facts and details conceptually, develop mnemonic strategies for memorizing them. Mnemonics can also help you retain and recall sequential processes.

Analyzers (ISTP and INTP)

Analyzers are interested in examining new information. You are comfortable in learning settings that allow you to critique and question what you are learning. You may feel confined and frustrated in overly structured or inflexible learning settings. Analyzers are drawn to opportunities to learn independently and enjoy self-study options when they have access to accurate and logically organized materials. If you plan to learn in a classroom setting, make sure you have expert and competent instruction. If the instructor does not know the subject, you may detach from the learning. Similarly, dogmatic material or approaches may not hold your interest. Take time alone before class to preview and process the learning materials. Ask your questions during breaks to avoid disrupting the flow of the class, or set up a question-and-answer session with a subject-area expert. Schedule time just before deadlines to accommodate your "just in time" style. Start larger learning projects, such as papers or reports, early to avoid last-minute stress. When working on group projects, see if you can work on a portion of the project independently.

Enhancers (ISFP and INFP)

Enhancers are interested in learning that is personally meaningful. Seek mentors, coaches, or tutors who can provide you with personalized and individualized learning materials, activities, interactions, and feedback. Taking on coaching and tutoring roles may also help you reinforce your learning. You may be uncomfortable in highly structured or impersonal learning settings. Look for opportunities to learn in flexible, supportive, collaborative settings. Independent learning may also appeal to you, especially if you have opportunities to work one-to-one with a supportive coach or co-learner as needed. You may work well under time pressure. If so, schedule time to complete learning tasks at the last minute. Consider organizing your time and tasks to accomplish goals a bit earlier, so you can avoid unforeseen last-minute circumstances. Because you focus on others' needs, you may find it hard to allow yourself time for learning. Say no to requests and let others know when you need uninterrupted learning time. When you receive frank, objective feedback, see this information as a valuable learning tool rather than a personal attack.

Reflection and Action

This chapter shows why it's essential to cultivate your curiosity. Lifelong learners who build skills and develop expertise throughout their career are valued in the workplace. Are you currently cultivating your curiosity by seeking out new information, managing information effectively, learning how to learn, and applying your learning to your day-to-day activities? Look at your responses to the checklists in the chapter and think about the suggestions offered. In the area below, write out some steps you can take to improve your ability to cultivate your curiosity.

CHAPTER EIGHT

Disentangle Your Thoughts

Clear thinking facilitates career success. Disentangling your thoughts involves selecting the right approach, strategies, and tools when you work on a particular task, make decisions, or solve problems. When you disentangle your thoughts, you organize and apply your thinking to manage situations effectively. You use a well-defined, systematic approach to solve problems and make decisions. You monitor and adjust your behaviors and strategies to ensure your success.

When you have trouble solving a problem, you determine why the blockage has occurred and decide how to move forward. As a result, others trust you to make well-thought-out decisions and solve problems effectively. They see you as resourceful and strategic. You adapt and flex your thought processes to respond to the situation at hand.

If you don't clarify and disentangle your thoughts, you may make impulsive or speculative decisions that can have a variety of negative consequences. Spur-of-the-moment decisions can lead to wasted resources, unhappy or resistant coworkers, and less than optimal results.

Similarly, a trial-and-error or unsystematic problem-solving strategy can mean ineffective work practices and wasted time and energy. If you use a haphazard or passive approach when making a decision or solving a problem, others will doubt your fitness to take on new challenges or manage situations. They will be less likely to recommend you for new opportunities or choose you for promotions.

Success Story: What Happened?

Workers who don't take a systematic approach to problem solving may face negative consequences. A construction supervisor describes the approach used by an apprentice. The apprentice was installing a shower enclosure on the second floor of a house. His supervisor noticed a leak in the ceiling directly below. When he pointed out the leak, the apprentice insisted he could not have caused the leak because he hadn't changed any of the plumbing. When the supervisor explored the situation more thoroughly, he discovered that the apprentice had fastened a screw into a water line inside the wall. The apprentice was surprised to learn that there was a link between leaking water and his actions, even though there was no other logical explanation. The supervisor used this teachable moment to encourage the apprentice to use systematic problem solving.

Are You an Effective Problem Solver?

The two lists that follow show the difference between effective and ineffective problem solving. Assess yourself by checking off the statements that best summarize your approach. If you check off statements in the first list, look for ways to minimize these behaviors by focusing on the positive behaviors in the second list.

Evidence of a haphazard or passive approach to problem solving

☐ Taking little time or energy to assess a problem
☐ Attempting several solutions using a trial-and-error approach
☐ Finding a "quick fix" rather than focusing on the cause of the problem
☐ Considering only one or two possible solutions
☐ Implementing a solution before analyzing the various consequences

- ☐ Lacking follow-through to implement a solution
- ☐ Neglecting to evaluate and adjust solutions or decisions as necessary
- ☐ Having a history of making many unsuccessful decisions

Evidence of systematic problem solving

- ☐ Taking time and energy to focus on a problem
- ☐ Using a well-defined, systematic approach
- ☐ Seeking the root cause of problems
- ☐ Considering and researching multiple solutions
- ☐ Analyzing the logical consequences for each solution
- ☐ Making and following through with a well-thought-out plan
- ☐ Evaluating results
- ☐ Adjusting your plan to improve results when necessary

The following section provides a series of steps for effective problem solving. The questions in each step emphasize the importance of clarifying your thinking when you tackle problems. Seek the insights and opinions of others who are involved in the problem. They may see blind spots or provide alternative options or perspectives you have not considered.

Step 1: Define the problem

Sometimes people don't look carefully at a problem; they try to find a quick fix that ignores underlying issues. This is like shooing flies. The fly moves away for a moment, but then it comes right back. If you only deal with the symptoms of a problem, the problem still remains. For example, you can ignore a person you don't get along with or cover up a mistake. These strategies may work well in the moment, but they won't solve your problems in the long run.

When you carefully define a problem, you can identify root causes rather than simply focusing on symptoms or creating a quick fix. By defining the problem, you can figure out exactly what you want to fix and envision success. This may seem like a lot of initial work, but it's well worth it; understanding what you want to change makes it much easier to come up with an effective solution. Answering the following questions can help you define the problem.

Clarify the problem

- How do I know there is a problem?
- How can I accurately describe the problem?
- Is the problem important?

Define ownership

- Does the problem need to be solved?
- Do I need to solve the problem?
- Who else is involved and how much ownership do they have in the problem?

Broaden your perspective

- Am I considering all aspects and possible causes of the problem?
- Am I getting distracted or sidetracked by other related problems or issues?
- How can I separate the problem from related problems or issues?
- Do I need to deal with any other related problems or issues?

Target the causes

- What is the root, or main, cause of the problem?
- Is there more than one cause?
- Which root cause is most important to address?

Define success

- Is there an opportunity in the problem?
- What will be the result of solving the problem?
- How will I know I am successful in solving the problem?
- What will I measure?

Step 2: Generate and research solutions

Problem situations usually feel uncomfortable, so you may be tempted to either avoid them or jump in with a solution. However, the best solution may not be the first one that comes to mind. If you want to solve a problem effectively, take time to generate and research a number of possible solutions. This is a good time to be creative. Look at the problem and potential solutions and outcomes from different perspectives. Use the following questions to stimulate your thinking.

- What are possible solutions to this problem?
- Can I look at this problem from a different perspective?
- If I change my perspective, might other solutions be possible?
- Am I being sufficiently open-minded when generating possible solutions?
- Have all the parties involved in this problem shared their perspectives?
- How do I determine whether a particular solution works?
- What further information do I need and how can I find it?

Step 3: Choose a Solution

This is a decision-making step. To choose the best solution to your problem, you must systematically evaluate each of your options. Here are some questions to help you evaluate your options. (You will find more information on decision making in the next section of this chapter.)

- What are the advantages and disadvantages of each option?
- What resources will I need to implement each solution?
- What biases do I have that might influence my decision?
- Are my emotions affecting how I see the possible solutions?
- What criteria should I use for making the decision and why?
- Am I considering both short-term and long-term effects and consequences?
- Am I balancing the needs of the people involved with the requirements of the task?

Step 4: Implement the Solution

Sometimes you know how to solve a problem, but lack the follow-through to achieve results. Make a concrete plan listing the steps you need to take and a timeline for achieving them. The plan will ensure that you put your solution into action. Use the following questions to stimulate your thinking about how to best implement your solution.

- What steps should I take to implement the solution?
- What are the roadblocks and how can I get around them?
- Am I getting distracted or sidetracked by other problems or issues?
- Do I need to deal with any other related problems or issues before implementing this solution?

Step 5: Evaluate the Results

After implementing your solution, make sure you've dealt with the problem successfully. If not, you may need to fine-tune your solution or rethink your problem-solving efforts. Evaluating your results will also help you assess and improve your problem-solving strategy. For example, suppose you discover that your problem solving didn't work because you forgot to consider the perspectives of the other people involved, or you were too optimistic about what you could accomplish. This information can help you solve your next problem. In this case, you can improve your problem-solving approach by seeking more input from others or making a more realistic timeline.

After you implement a solution to a problem, evaluate your results by answering the following questions.

- Did I solve the problem?
- Did I solve it in the best way possible?
- What lessons did I learn?
- What might I do differently next time?
- Am I capitalizing on potential opportunities?
- How can I keep this problem from happening again?
- Which parts of the problem-solving process worked well?
- Are there parts of the problem-solving process I need to improve?

When you deal with difficult situations, strive to see challenges and roadblocks as possibilities, not problems. These not-planned-for events allow you to find new approaches and improve situations. When you reframe situations positively, you can look for alternative ways of operating to enhance your results. Although we call this process *problem solving*, you can use it to create or capitalize on an opportunity as well as to solve a problem.

Excel Your Way: Tips for Extraverted (E) and Introverted (I) types

If you have a preference for Extraversion (E), you may be tempted to move quickly toward implementing a solution when solving a problem. Taking more time to clarify the problem and generate possible solutions before acting helps you avoid trial-and-error problem-solving attempts.

If you have a preference for Introversion (I), you may naturally take time to clarify problems and research solutions. This results in well-thought-out solutions. At times, you may need to move more quickly to the implementation stage of problem solving to ensure that problems are dealt with promptly.

Are You an Effective Decision Maker?

Life is full of decisions. Some may seem small and unimportant; others may have enormous consequences. Most people have experienced the consequences of a poor decision, and some people seem to consistently make poor choices. Using a systematic approach when making decisions increases your chances of career success and helps you avoid the consequences of poor choices.

The decision-making process below works for any situation, no matter what the scale of the decision. The decision-making and problem-solving processes overlap considerably. Both require you to systematically work through a process and choose the most appropriate course of action. The questions in each step help to clarify your thinking during the decision-making process. As you read through the steps, think about your decision-making process and look for ways to refine and improve it.

Step 1: Clarify the situation

- Do I need to make a decision?
- What, exactly, do I need to decide?

- What will happen if I don't make a decision?
- What are my timelines? Are they adequate?

Step 2: Identify alternatives

- Am I using a broad perspective to identify all possible options?
- Do I need to do any preliminary research to identify additional options?
- Have I sought the input of other people who will be affected by the decision?

Step 3: Set and evaluate the decision-making criteria

- Have I established clear criteria for making this decision?
- Have I considered all the criteria pertaining to the decision?
- Have I ranked or otherwise prioritized my criteria?
- Have I considered how others will be affected by my decision?
- Have I considered including both objective and subjective criteria?

Step 4: Evaluate the alternatives and make a choice

- Do I have a way to measure how well each option meets the criteria?
- Have I done enough research to evaluate each alternative accurately?
- Have I followed each option through to its consequences and implications?
- Am I taking enough time to evaluate my decision?
- Does my choice accurately reflect the prioritized criteria?

Step 5: Reflect on and revisit the decision-making process

- Did I get the expected results from my decision?
- If I didn't achieve the results I expected, why not?
- What might I do differently next time?
- Did I navigate parts of the decision-making process effectively?
- Are there parts of the decision-making process I need to improve?

Although these steps may seem overly detailed, this systematic approach ensures that you are considering all aspects of your decision. Depending on the decision you need to make, you can complete the steps very quickly or over an extended period. For example, to decide what snack to eat, you need to consider how hungry you are and what food is available. Your criteria may include health concerns, energy needs, or desired taste. Then you can quickly prioritize these criteria.

For a more complex decision, such as a career choice, your decision-making process includes criteria such as interests, skills, values, aptitudes, personality, constraints, and lifestyle. You may have numerous options that require extensive research. You may want to consider how work choices affect your family or significant others as well as yourself.

The reflection step of decision making may entail thinking back through a number of work decisions and sorting out what worked well and what didn't. Give yourself sufficient time to work through complex decisions. After you make a choice, you can evaluate whether that choice worked well. This information can help you make a better choice next time.

Can You Identify Your Blind Spots?

Here are some common blind spots in problem solving and decision making. Read through them and think about whether they apply to you. If so, try implementing the tips provided.

Tunnel vision

People sometimes suffer from tunnel vision when they set out to define problems, clarify situations, and identify alternatives or possible solutions. If you tend to see only one solution to a problem, make immediate decisions, or see limited options for a decision, you may have this blind spot. Immediate decisions can be efficient, and sometimes they are necessary; however, making a decision or solving a problem too quickly eliminates options and opportunities. Sometimes the best option or solution is the one you don't see immediately.

If you think this blind spot applies to you, take time to think "outside the box" and consider your problem or decision from broad perspectives. Enlist others to help you see the situation in alternate ways. Identify and challenge your assumptions. For example, if you are trying to decide which car to buy, consider whether you really need a car. Maybe you could join a car pool, walk, bike, rent or lease a car, or use public transit. By expanding your options, you will find more opportunities.

Excel Your Way:
Tips for Judging (J) and Perceiving (P) types

If you have a preference for Judging (J), you seek closure and are most comfortable after you make a decision and can move forward to accomplish goals. If you take more time to explore possibilities and consider various options before deciding, you may make a better decision.

If you have a preference for Perceiving (P), you like to explore and keep your options open. Making decisions and implementing solutions interest you less than exploring options. Sometimes you may need to reach closure more quickly so you can move forward and accomplish your goals.

Over- or under-including others in your decisions

Determine who should play a role in your problem-solving and decision-making processes. Decisions made with too little or too much consultation can create problems. Recognize when you need to make decisions quickly and independently and when you need to include others in the process.

You may tend to overlook others' needs when you make decisions or tackle problems. This may alienate coworkers; if so, they may not support your actions. On the other hand, if you try to please everyone when making a decision or solving a problem, you can end up immobilized.

Are you likely to consult others too much or too little? Do you need to find a different balance? If you are not considering others, start to ask for input and practice your listening skills. If you find yourself trying to please everyone, express your needs and separate them from the needs of others in the situation.

Excel Your Way:
Tips for Thinking (T) and Feeling (F) types

If you have a preference for Thinking (T), you are most comfortable creating clear, logical criteria for decision making. Improve your decision-making and problem-solving process by adding in a personal, subjective component.

If you have a preference for Feeling (F), you tend to tune in to the needs and situations of others. Improve your decision-making and problem-solving process by adding in an objective, logical analysis of the situation.

Defining and applying decision-making criteria

A key part of decision making is establishing clear criteria for evaluating options. If you find it difficult to make or stick to your decisions, this may be a blind spot. You also may have this blind spot if your criteria conflict. For example, if you want to take on extra roles and responsibilities at work to generate additional income, but you also want to maximize time with your family, you may be putting yourself in a lose-lose situation.

Success Story: Nothing Works

A tradesperson was torn between living close to work or spending time apart from his family. The highest paying jobs with the best benefits required travel away from home. Local work was harder to find and paid much less. Because he wanted both time with his family and high wages and benefits, he was constantly dissatisfied. At work, he wished he was back home; when he was home, he worried about income. When he realized his two criteria, high salary and being close to home, were incompatible in his line of work, he refocused his decision making.

If you find this a difficult step in the process, list and prioritize your criteria. Look for possible conflicts. Discussing your criteria, especially with people who are involved in and affected by your decisions, will help clarify your thought process. Others can also offer experienced perspectives on the potential pros and cons of your options.

When evaluating and choosing an alternative based on the decision-making criteria, focus on logical outcomes. Think of both short- and long-term consequences for each option. Mentally work through an option to its outcome before taking action. As well, consider the situations and needs of the people involved in your decision. This is an important balance. Overemphasis on either side can create problems.

Excel Your Way:
Tips for Sensing (S) and Intuitive (N) types

If you have a preference for Sensing (S), you may be more interested in considering the immediate than the long-term consequences of decisions. Improve your problem solving and decision making by also considering broader consequences of possible decisions or solutions.

If you have a preference for Intuition (N), you may be more interested in considering long-term than immediate consequences. Improve your problem solving and decision making by also considering short-term, practical consequences of possible decisions or solutions.

Are You Thinking About
Your Thinking?

There are many ways, or modes, of thinking. Each thinking mode may or may not be useful in a particular situation. To disentangle your thoughts, you need to know when to use different thinking modes. For example, when you are responding to an emergency, long-term strategic thinking is not the way to go. Or if you are using the creative thinking process to generate alternatives, you need to know when to shift to the evaluative process to select the best alternative. In the same way, you must learn when to turn off your critical analysis and become more open-minded about alternatives that appear unreasonable at first glance. Consciously evaluating and adjusting thinking processes is key to disentangling your thoughts.

Many books are devoted to discussing ways of thinking. For the purposes of this book, we will focus on five basic thinking modes: practical, creative, global, logical, and humanistic. Increasing your awareness of these modes will help you decide when and why to shift from one to another. Awareness is the starting point for balancing and refining your information processing, problem solving, and decision making.

The following checklists describe the five modes of thinking. Check off the statements that describe how you think. Consider circumstances in which you might use each mode.

Practical thinking

- ☐ Observing and cataloging facts related to a specific situation
- ☐ Choosing realistic and practical solutions to problems
- ☐ Making efficient decisions that take minimal effort to implement
- ☐ Making use of conventional wisdom and personal experience
- ☐ Adapting existing processes and strategies to the situation at hand

Creative thinking

- ☐ Sharing many ideas and possibilities
- ☐ Contributing ideas that are distinctly different from what others are sharing
- ☐ Finding alternative uses for common objects
- ☐ Presenting many original solutions for problems
- ☐ Providing many possible options when making decisions

Global thinking

- ☐ Identifying trends and patterns
- ☐ Describing long-term implications and consequences
- ☐ Finding links and connections between pieces of information
- ☐ Synthesizing information into an integrated, holistic form
- ☐ Focusing on whole systems and interactions rather than specific pieces

Logical thinking

- ☐ Analyzing and evaluating information
- ☐ Using objective reasoning to reach a conclusion
- ☐ Weighing the pros and cons of options
- ☐ Focusing on logical consequences and implications
- ☐ Describing cause-and-effect relationships

Humanistic thinking

- ☐ Weighing information using personal, subjective beliefs and values
- ☐ Assessing the effects of decisions and actions on the well-being of others
- ☐ Focusing on harmony and positive morale within a group
- ☐ Accommodating the likes, dislikes, and needs of others
- ☐ Acknowledging and appreciating others

The following section describes the five modes of thinking in more detail and provides some questions to hone your thinking and disentangle your thoughts.

Practical thinking

Alternative terms for practical thinking include *everyday thinking*, *realistic thinking*, *common sense*, and *conventional wisdom*. When you engage in practical thinking, you consider the realities of a situation and select the easiest and most pragmatic approach. Focusing on the realities, facts, and details of a situation is key to this mode of thinking. Here are some of the questions to ask when you engage in practical thinking.

- What facts and realities are relevant to the situation?
- Is the proposed solution or decision practical?
- Is there an easier way to do the task?
- Will my actions be successful?
- What has worked before?
- What have I learned from past experiences in this type of situation?
- How can I adapt what I know to deal with this situation?

Practical thinking requires a focus on the here and now. Practical thinking grounds you by providing a reality check for ideas and a concrete link to the facts and details related to a particular situation. Because practical thinking is focused on realities, it helps you accurately estimate what you can accomplish in a given period by breaking complex tasks into concrete, achievable units.

Sometimes people bypass this mode of thinking and become lost in theories and ideas, failing to link these abstractions to the immediate realities. If you tend to focus on ideas and theories, make a step-by-step plan to move from the current situation toward the ideas you envision. Analyze the gap between what is real and what you envision. Making observations or recording specific data will help you focus on realities and clarify what you need to achieve. Attend to details such as timelines, costs, and resources required. Observe and research current realities and find out about past attempts at solutions.

Creative thinking

You need to use both practical and creative thinking in your approach to most situations. It is important to balance the realities with the possibilities. If you minimize the realities, you won't be able to implement your solutions. If you don't consider the possibilities, you may miss out on opportunities.

Creative thinking also is called *divergent thinking, thinking "outside the box," generative thinking,* and *unconventional thinking.* Creative thinking uses processes such as brainstorming—suspending critical thoughts while generating as many ideas as possible. Strong creative thinkers can come up with many alternatives, especially original alternatives that show flexibility of thought. If you have flexibility of thought, you find unusual uses for objects, change and redefine the contexts of problems, and view situations from diverse perspectives. Here are some questions to ask when engaging in creative thinking.

- What other topics might connect with this topic?
- How can I look at this situation differently?
- What is the second, third, or fourth right answer?
- What other options can I consider?
- How can I sidestep restrictions that limit my thinking?

Creative thinking enables you to see new and different ways of approaching situations and solving problems. When you use creative thinking, you envision changes and new ways of doing things. Creative thinking allows you to see what could be. It can help you imagine future possibilities or find innovative ways to deal with realities.

Not everyone is comfortable using this mode of thinking. Some people see the creative thinking process as unrealistic daydreaming. If you are most comfortable with practical thinking, you may have trouble imagining what you have not experienced. Find practical reasons for suspending the restrictions of reality. For example, you may be more willing to engage in creative thinking if you see it as a useful step for evaluating and choosing options. If you are grounded in practical thinking, you may find it easiest to move into creative thinking by making a series of incremental changes. Take small steps toward using your imagination. Think about aspects of past situations to help you create alternative ideas for the current situation.

Excel Your Way: Tips for Sensing (S) and Intuitive (N) types

If you have a preference for Sensing (S), you enjoy spontaneously adapting your creativity to practical uses. For example, a Sensing type thinking "outside the box" may use materials at hand to jury-rig a stalled car's gas line and reach the destination.

If you have a preference for Intuition (N), you enjoy inventing a totally new way of doing something. For example, an Intuitive type thinking "outside the box" may discover alternative ways to arrive at his or her destination without using the car.

You are most creative when you predict possible events, improvise alternative solutions to problems, or generate new ideas. Finding original ways of thinking about a situation opens the door to new possibilities. You may develop a more effective procedure to accomplish a task or use a new idea to improve an existing process. You might adapt existing objects and ideas to create a new result. For example, you may use the organization's existing resources to create an alternative and practical solution to an old problem. Taking a broad view of the situation allows you to be more proactive in your approach. Creative activities such as free association, brainstorming, and other forms of outside-the-box thinking can help you compose innovative solutions to problems.

Global thinking

Global thinking is also called *futuristic thinking*, *systems thinking*, and *integrative thinking*. Global thinking focuses on the future and on integrating components and systems into a holistic framework. It is a long-term, big-picture approach. You may see global thinking as the exclusive responsibility of top management, but in fact, everyone benefits from understanding and working toward broader goals and visions.

Global thinking allows you to see situations from broad perspectives. When you look at a small part of something, it is easy to miss many of the interactions and links to other parts of the system. The result may be shortsighted problem solving and decision making. Here are some questions to ask when engaging in global thinking.

- What are the long-term effects and consequences of our actions?
- What parts of the whole system will be involved?
- What are our long-term goals?
- Are my current actions moving us toward the long-term goals?
- What is the vision for the future?
- What will the system look like when the vision is implemented?
- How do relevant systems and processes interact and interface?

When you use global thinking, you choose from unlimited possibilities and see implications beyond the current situation. This mode of thinking connects to creative and logical thinking. For example, some creative thinking is involved when formulating a vision, and some assessment of logical consequences is involved when looking at long-range effects. However, the defining element of global thinking is the integrative, long-term aspect.

Excel Your Way:
Tips for Sensing (S) and Intuitive (N) types

If you have a preference for Sensing (S), you naturally tend to use practical thinking. You enjoy using creative thinking in the moment to solve an immediate problem. Challenge yourself to use global thinking to find long-term as well as short-term adaptive solutions. Identify patterns and trends from past experience and use them, along with current data, to predict future developments and develop your global thinking.

If you have a preference for Intuition (N), you are attracted to creative and global thinking. Practical thinking may be less interesting for you. Challenge yourself to use practical thinking to react in immediate situations and global and creative thinking to develop long-range ideas and solutions. Align your immediate reactions to your long-term goals.

Logical thinking

Logical thinking also is referred to as *analytic thinking, critical thinking, tactical thinking, objective thinking*, and *strategic thinking*. Logical thinking involves analyzing, evaluating, and making judgments about information. This mode of thinking usually results in a critical evaluation or in a logical plan or solution. Here are some questions to ask when engaging in logical thinking.

- Why is this situation happening?
- What is causing this situation?
- What will be the logical consequences of action or inaction?
- What are the pros and cons of various objectives?
- What is the logical thing to do?
- What are the criteria for a solution or decision?
- What solution or decision best matches the criteria?

Logical thinking helps you evaluate situations. To think logically, you must minimize personal biases and view situations as objectively as possible. Some people find it difficult to engage in logical thinking and tend to make errors when they try to use this mode. To use logical thinking effectively, you must make accurate assumptions and recognize faulty arguments. To develop this thinking mode, look for the reasoning behind your conclusions and explore your assumptions when you evaluate information or situations. When making decisions or solving problems, clarify and list your criteria. This will help you evaluate the situation more objectively. Analyze arguments to detect inconsistencies and biases.

Success Story: That's Not Going to Work

This story demonstrates the importance of using critical thinking at the right time. A team member with ISTP personality type preferences was very adept at pointing out flaws. His team became frustrated with him during brainstorming sessions. Rather than generating ideas in these sessions, he was mostly quiet, yet he was quick to dismiss illogical or impractical ideas. After his team talked to him about his behavior, he began using more open-ended creative thinking and refrained from evaluating ideas until the end of each brainstorming session. As a result, his coworkers found the brainstorming process much easier. After the brainstorming ended, and they began to evaluate options, the team was eager to hear their coworker's critiques.

Humanistic thinking

Humanistic thinking also is referred to as *emotional intelligence*, *values-based thinking*, and *subjective thinking*. When you use humanistic thinking, you prioritize human values and personal responses. Humanistic thinkers consider how people are affected by information rather than simply focusing on the information itself. Humanistic thinkers accommodate people's needs and thus generate goodwill. Here are some questions to ask when you engage in humanistic thinking.

- Who is affected by the issue?
- How do people feel about it?
- Will anyone be hurt?
- Is the situation fair to everyone involved? Is everyone being considered?
- Will changes make things better or worse for the people involved?

- How will the workplace atmosphere or morale be affected?
- How will this situation affect my relationships with the people involved?

Like logical thinking, humanistic thinking helps you evaluate situations. But humanistic thinking considers the personal and subjective, rather than the impersonal and objective, side of situations. Some people are naturally drawn to gathering humanistic information, and others are not.

   If you find it difficult to gather and interpret humanistic information, start by directly asking people how a situation affects them. Listen carefully to their answers and imagine the situation from their perspective. But don't stop there, or you may make erroneous assumptions. Use the summarizing techniques in Chapter 5 to see if you understand others' perspectives. When you develop criteria for decision making or problem solving, think about how decisions will affect the people involved.

Excel Your Way: Tips for Thinking (T) and Feeling (F) types

If you have a preference for Thinking (T), you naturally are drawn to logical thinking. You may need to balance your objective analysis of situations by also using humanistic thinking.

   If you have a preference for Feeling (F), you naturally are drawn to humanistic thinking. You may need to balance your subjective consideration of people by also using logical thinking.

Disentangling Your Thoughts: Personality Type Strengths and Challenges

All personality types can improve their career success by disentangling their thoughts. Every personality type has unique strengths and challenges aligned to their natural preferences. Read through the information on your personality type for suggestions specifically tailored to your natural way of working.

Responders (ESTP and ESFP)

Responders tend to use their thinking in the here and now. You like identifying immediate problems and looking for practical solutions. You concentrate on the known, relevant facts and are less inclined to look for answers by reviewing the past in detail. You use your creative thinking to adapt in the moment. At times, you might be tempted to make a quick fix to get things up and running instead of taking the time to identify root causes and long-term solutions. Similarly, you may be more interested in trying something for now to see how it works than in looking at longer-term consequences and implications. You may grow impatient when others discuss strategic or global approaches. Know when to move your thinking out of the moment to look backward and forward in time. As you solve problems and make decisions, look for patterns from the past and project what will happen in the future.

Explorers (ENTP and ENFP)

Explorers tend to use creative and global thinking to consider unusual solutions to problems. Your preferences help you imagine many interesting and motivating options and choices. Because you prefer to keep your options open and explore possibilities, you may find decision making confining rather than comfortable. Explorers also may be less interested in implementing a solution than in moving on to a new problem or idea. Recognize when it's best to be decisive. In these situations challenge yourself to reach closure, take action, and follow through with a solution or decision. You likely think strategically and take a global, long-term approach when solving problems and making decisions. You also may feel confined by practical thinking. Seeing the facts and details of the situation is less interesting for you than imagining options and possibilities for the future. Learn to incorporate practical as well as creative thinking into your work to build a greater awareness of the realities and practicalities of a situation. Practical thinking can help you translate your ideas and vision into action.

Expeditors (ESTJ and ENTJ)

When solving problems, Expeditors tend to use logical thinking and seek expedient solutions. You like to make your decisions as quickly as possible. Logical decisiveness is useful and efficient in many situations, but it can interfere with creative thinking. By deciding quickly, you may miss solutions and options that aren't apparent at first glance. Use creative and global thinking before engaging in logical thinking to ensure that you consider alternatives. When you make decisions quickly, you may also miss out on other's input. If you dismiss, or fail to seek, such input, coworkers may grow unsupportive, which may negatively affect your ability to address the problem or decision at hand. Although you are not naturally drawn to humanistic thinking, it's essential when you work with others, especially those who have a preference for Feeling. When making your decisions, incorporate personal criteria and consequences into your logical thinking process.

Contributors (ESFJ and ENFJ)

Contributors are attracted to humanistic thinking and are interested in understanding how situations affect individuals. You prefer to collaborate and cooperate with others when solving problems and making decisions, because what others want and need is of great importance to you. Although it's useful to look at the human side of situations, at times you need to take a logical approach to solving a problem or making a decision. This is especially important when you need to justify spending resources on a goal or project. Although you may not be drawn to logical thinking, you can learn to approach situations more objectively by analyzing the pros and cons of options and focusing on logical consequences and implications. Because you are interested in maintaining harmony, you tend to place less emphasis on your own needs when making decisions and solving problems. Over time, this tendency may make you resentful and dissatisfied. Prevent negative feelings by including your own needs as well as others' in your decision-making criteria. Balancing logical and humanistic thinking enables you to consider both the personal and logical implications of situations.

Assimilators (ISTJ and ISFJ)

Assimilators are attracted to practical thinking and maintaining status quo. You prefer structured and predictable situations with clear expectations. When situations require problem solving and decision making, you tend to take a cautious approach. You want to know the relevant facts, so when you set out to solve a problem you think back to what worked in the past. Looking back may help you address current problems, but being overly dependent on previous solutions can limit your opportunity to view situations from different perspectives. Sometimes the traditional, tried-and-true solution does not provide the result you need. If you find yourself consistently making decisions that preserve the status quo, you may be hampered by your cautious and conservative approach. Practice using global and creative thinking to anticipate the future and imagine alternative options or solutions. These two modes of thinking help you remain open to new ideas and perspectives.

Visionaries (INTJ and INFJ)

Visionaries are especially drawn to global and creative thinking. You use these thinking approaches to consider a wide range of options and long-term implications and consequences when solving problems and making decisions. You want to make decisions and take action, but you also want to explore problems in depth; that may leave you facing some difficult choices. At some point you need to limit the possibilities and start taking action. Taking time to clearly define problems will help you manage your problem-solving and decision-making processes. Avoid trying to integrate all aspects of complex situations or attempting to solve multiple problems with one solution. Use practical thinking to tease problems into smaller parts and implement workable solutions to these smaller problems. Though tempting, it is not practical to address multiple problems at one time.

Analyzers (ISTP and INTP)

Analyzers use logical thinking to examine and evaluate problems and decisions. You are attracted to solving problems and determining why a problem has occurred. Implementing solutions doesn't interest you as much, so you may need to motivate yourself to follow through. Your calm, objective, logical approach has several advantages, especially when you are dealing with emergency situations. However, your approach leaves little room for the more personal aspects of problem solving and decision making. You may lose others' goodwill and cooperation when you take a purely logical approach to problems. Although you are not naturally drawn to humanistic thinking, it can help you process the personal aspects of situations. Considering and accommodating others' needs and wants will result in a more satisfactory solution for everyone.

Enhancers (ISFP and INFP)

Enhancers are attracted to humanistic thinking and are careful to consider others' needs and perspectives when solving problems and making decisions. However, you tend to put others' needs and wants ahead of your own. In these situations, your solutions may accommodate others at the risk of ignoring your own wants and needs. Using this approach over time may lead to resentment and frustration. Don't assume others will, in turn, think about *your* needs. You need to give yourself equal consideration when evaluating and choosing solutions. Using logical thinking helps you step back and see the objective as well as the personal side of situations.

Reflection and Action

This chapter shows why it's essential to disentangle your thoughts. When you organize and structure your thinking, you can take a well-informed approach to problem solving and decision making. Effective problem solvers and decision makers are prized in the workplace. This chapter also describes how to move in and out of different thinking modes. Aligning your thinking mode to the situation at hand helps you react appropriately and provides the mental flexibility you need to excel at work. Look at your responses to the checklists and think about the suggestions offered. In the area below, write out some steps you can take to improve your ability to disentangle your thoughts.

CHAPTER NINE

· ·

Exceed Expectations

*T*o achieve career success, you must convince people that you will exceed their expectations and achieve exceptional results. To exceed expectations you prioritize, plan, organize your time and activities, and persist on tasks at hand to complete work efficiently. You continuously look for ways to be more effective as you strive to meet and exceed the expectations laid out for you. You show pride in your work and take initiative.

When you exceed expectations, others see you as results oriented, productive, persistent, efficient, and effective. They trust you will complete your work and do it well. When others know you will do a good job, they feel confident offering you new and important tasks and projects.

When workers do not meet expectations, employers see them as disorganized, inefficient, easily distracted, or underachieving. Such employees coast through the workday without giving their tasks the time and energy they require; as a result, their work is frequently incomplete or behind schedule. Employers lose confidence in workers who do not meet expectations. Even if they don't lose their jobs, such workers are unlikely to be considered for promotion.

Are You Productive at Work?

To achieve results and exceed expectations, you first must be productive. And to be productive, you need to establish priorities. When your priorities are clear, you can plan and organize your tasks and time to achieve results effectively.

If you do not plan and organize your time and tasks, you may rush from one task to another, always feeling behind or unprepared. At times, everyone struggles to meet their obligations. But productive individuals prioritize, plan, and organize to help them stay on top of their work. Read the following checklists to determine if you are taking a productive approach to work. Check off the statements describing your approach. The next section shows you how to prioritize, plan, and organize more effectively in order to achieve results.

Evidence of an unorganized and inefficient approach to work

- [ ] Reacting in the moment rather than working toward goals
- [ ] Being unsure of priorities
- [ ] Spending significant time or energy on unimportant activities
- [ ] Missing deadlines
- [ ] Completing tasks in a last-minute rush that reduces quality
- [ ] Being unprepared for meetings or discussions

Evidence of prioritizing, planning, and organizing

- [ ] Setting goals
- [ ] Identifying and working on the most important tasks first
- [ ] Making and following a plan to accomplish important goals
- [ ] Meeting deadlines
- [ ] Completing tasks on time while maintaining quality
- [ ] Being prepared for meetings or discussions

Prioritizing and planning

Establishing priorities has many advantages. Taking time to inventory your various tasks, objectives, and goals makes it easier to see all your responsibilities. When you establish priorities, you can more easily focus on the task at hand, knowing that you will address each task in order of priority. Once you know what to do and when to do it, you can provide realistic timelines for completing your work. Clarify your priorities with others; you may need to negotiate if their priorities and expectations conflict with your own.

To establish priorities, first list all the tasks you need to do and rank their importance based on your goals, values, or deadlines. When prioritizing and planning, ask yourself why certain tasks and goals are more important than others. Consider both immediate, deadline-driven tasks—the kind that often take all your time and energy—and less urgent work, including strategic, global goals. After establishing priorities, plan your actions by sequencing tasks and setting timelines.

Initiate a conversation about priorities and expectations with your supervisor or leader. Work-performance issues occur when employees and employers have differing priorities. Clarifying what others expect will help determine your priorities.

Excel Your Way: Tips for Sensing (S) and Intuitive (N) types

If you have a preference for Sensing (S), you are attracted to acting in the moment and setting practical goals and priorities. For you, long-term goals are less compelling than immediate outcomes. Try adjusting your priorities to address longer-term goals. This will balance your practical approach with a broader perspective.

If you have a preference for Intuition (N), you are stimulated by activities aligned with long-term visions and goals. Adjust your priorities to address shorter-term goals. This will help meet the demands of your current situation.

Balance your planning with action. If you spend too much time listing and prioritizing every last task, including even the smallest items, you may lose an opportunity to act in the moment. Sometimes the most time-efficient approach is simply to make a call or complete a task rather than write down and integrate the activity into a planning process. However, if you constantly respond to immediate requests, you won't have time for more important but less urgent tasks. Carefully consider how to attend to both immediate and long-range tasks and goals.

For example, suppose you read e-mail but don't reply immediately. Over time, you will amass a large backlog of messages awaiting your response. But if you respond to e-mail more frequently, you'll have less time to focus on and complete other tasks. Setting aside a specific time for e-mail may be the best solution. The challenge is to maximize your efforts in the moment while also planning and prioritizing.

When you have decided which tasks are your highest priorities, make an action plan. Use a planning system; this can be anything from pencil and paper to a software program or electronic organizer. Planning systems can help you manage your day, week, month, year, or life. There are both project and contract management systems. It doesn't matter what system you use; what matters is taking a systematic process to planning your actions. Here are some tips for prioritizing and planning.

- Align your priorities to your goals.
- List your daily activities. Break goals into small tasks and include only the tasks you can complete that day. Avoid making lists of goals that may take weeks, even months, to complete. These lists become frustrating because you rarely enjoy the satisfaction of completing a task.
- Make sure the tasks on your daily to-do list are high priority, specific, and achievable.
- Reward yourself with a short break when you complete a task.

Excel Your Way: Tips for Judging (J) and Perceiving (P) types

If you have a preference for Judging (J), you are probably comfortable structuring and organizing tasks. Use your natural strengths to evaluate and choose the best planning and organizing system to deal with your priorities and information.

If you have a preference for Perceiving (P), you may not enjoy planning and organizing. Use a flexible planning system to create a basic structure for organizing your tasks and meeting deadlines.

Organization

Setting priorities and planning are the first steps to productivity. The next step is organization. Being disorganized wastes time, energy, and resources, and it can doom your best-laid plans to failure. By becoming more organized, you will minimize distractions and work effectively.

Dealing with information inefficiently is a major time waster. At work you likely are deluged with memos, articles, agendas, files, reports, newsletters, updates, and customer or client data, as well as e-mail, URLs, and text and voice messages—all of which you need to organize and manage. You want to be able to access this information without being distracted from your priorities. If you can't find important information, miss meetings or opportunities to respond to timely issues, or complain you were not aware of information that has already been distributed, you need to get organized.

Create and follow a plan for dealing with information. For example, if e-mail or text messages contain a meeting date, immediately record the details in a planner. (Perhaps your software will help by adding meetings to your schedule.) Avoid the temptation to organize information later rather than sooner. After you adopt or create a system for organizing time and tasks, use it every day. Here are some tips.

- Put materials and resources in designated spots.
- Use notebooks, folders, or a briefcase if you tend to misplace paperwork.
- If you deal with a lot of information, establish a filing system to minimize the time you spend looking for things.
- Try one new organizing strategy at a time.

Success Story: Method to the Madness

As the following example illustrates, people use different strategies for organizing. An office manager with ENTP personality type preferences never stored files in a filing cabinet until projects were completed. Instead, she had "project piles" of binders and files in her office. Her coworkers considered her disorganized. Rather than accept the negative label, she encouraged them to see her as a "conceptual organizer." She explained that she grouped everything she needed for a given project. When she had time to work on a project, she took the project pile to her desk; then she could work on tasks efficiently and effectively. When she explained her method, others saw the order in her apparent disorganization.

Finding supplies and other workplace resources can be a big time waster. How much time do you spend looking for a stapler, staples, pens, paper, a reference book, or other supplies? Are the tools and equipment you need handy? Organize your workspace. Minimize the distraction of searching for items, especially those you use often.

You can also improve organization by having all of your tools and equipment in good repair. Using an unreliable stapler or typing on a sticky keyboard wastes your time. Regular maintenance will keep your tools and equipment in optimal condition. In the long run, you will save time and energy that would be lost fixing equipment or waiting for repairs.

Make your workspace a comfortable and efficient place to accomplish tasks. Ergonomic chairs, desks, lights, and workstations maximize comfort and minimize physical distractions. Design your workspace to facilitate your most frequent tasks. If you often use something, keep it close and easily accessible.

Communication is essential in the workplace, yet unnecessary communication can distract you or others and interfere with task completion. Determine whether you are effectively planning, organizing, and completing your communications. Organize your workspace to minimize interruptions.

Excel Your Way: Tips for Extroverted (E) and Introverted (I) types

If you have a preference for Extroversion (E), you enjoy interacting and discussing work tasks with others. Rather than communicating with others frequently, save some topics for a later conversation. This will help you complete tasks as well as minimize interruptions to yourself and others.

If you have a preference for Introversion (I), you may find it difficult to regain your concentration after being interrupted. To complete a task without interruption, you may need to use cues such as a closed door to let coworkers know when you are unavailable for discussion.

Here are some practical suggestions for organizing your workspace.

To make a space quiet

- Shut your door
- Use earplugs
- Ask the people making noise to be quiet
- Turn off your phone

To make a space comfortable

- Change or adjust the chair
- Change or adjust the table or desk
- Control the heat, light, and glare if possible
- Hang or rearrange posters or pictures on the walls

To make a space practical

- Find the most efficient arrangement for your computer, desk, chair, and other furniture
- Lose clutter—especially clutter unrelated to the work at hand
- Organize work materials
- Keep work materials within easy reach

Managing procrastination

When you procrastinate, you leave tasks unstarted or incomplete. However, sometimes an incomplete task simply means you reestablished your priorities. Know the difference between effectively setting priorities and procrastinating. For example, if you have a strong urge to sort your rarely used bottom desk drawer before finishing a lengthy inventory report due tomorrow morning, you are probably procrastinating. If you ignore an unimportant e-mail, you are prioritizing, not procrastinating. When you procrastinate, explore why, and then deal with the reason directly.

Reasons for procrastinating include

- Not knowing what to do or how to do it
- Lacking the skills or tools to proceed

- Being distracted from or uninterested in the task
- Feeling too tired, stressed, ill, unfit, or lethargic
- Fearing failure
- Fearing success
- Being indecisive
- Failing to establish clear priorities
- Being unwilling to start a task there isn't time to finish
- Being unwilling to start a task for fear it won't get done perfectly

When you have identified the reason you are not attending to tasks, use your problem-solving strategy from Chapter 8 to tackle the problem. For example, if you are procrastinating because you are distracted, find the source of your distraction and eliminate it. If you are unwilling to start a complex task, break it into smaller, more manageable pieces. Avoiding procrastination and managing your time, information, and resources by prioritizing, planning, and organizing are the first steps in a productive approach to work.

Do You Achieve Exceptional Results?

Prioritizing, planning, and organizing provide the starting point for exceeding expectations, but these tools alone are not enough. You must also complete your work at a higher standard than expected and continuously improve your work.

Clarifying expectations and standards

If you don't know what people want, it is impossible to meet their expectations. It isn't always easy to find out what is expected of you. Some work standards are simple and concrete, such as arriving on time; others are complex, such as completing all phases of a complicated project within scheduled timelines.

It is your responsibility to clearly define work expectations and standards. Written job descriptions sometimes outline these expectations, but they can be ambiguous. They tend to list roles you are responsible for, but fail to include specific standards for those roles. You may need to clarify expectations and standards with your supervisor or leader. Otherwise you may not perform as expected simply because you are not aware of your supervisor's expectations.

Identifying and listing criteria will help you demonstrate that you are completing work to accepted standards. You can also ask a supervisor, leader, or expert for feedback on your performance. Carefully listen to comments about the quality of your efforts. Ask for or observe examples of high-quality work. For example, when writing a report, find and refer to a well-written sample. Learn about and apply standards from outside your organization, such as health and safety regulations and other mandatory requirements.

Excel Your Way:
Tips for Thinking (T) and Feeling (F) types

If you have a preference for Thinking (T), you likely emphasize work products when defining standards. Use this tendency to clearly define criteria and standards for producing high-quality work. Then develop work standards to facilitate teamwork and positive interactions.

If you have a preference for Feeling (F), you likely emphasize teamwork and interactions when defining standards. Use this tendency to clearly define criteria and standards for building effective work relationships. Then develop clear objective criteria to ensure work product excellence.

Maintain a balance between independence and collaboration. If you constantly check in with others to determine their expectations, you'll be a drain on their time and energy and will come across as overly dependent. Simply find out enough information to set your standards and then strive to meet them.

Success Story: The New Guy

The following example demonstrates the importance of clarifying expectations. A plant operator saw himself as "the new guy" even though he had been on the job for well over a year. He consulted the experts—workers with more than five years experience—whenever problems arose. He was surprised to learn that others thought he was not working up to standard. When he realized that management expected him to take more initiative in solving problems, he immediately changed his behavior. He still consults the experts when he has difficult questions, but he stopped relying on them to take a lead role in solving problems.

Standards, like any desired outcome, are most effective when they are measurable. For example, if you work in a restaurant, spell out the criteria you use to define exceptional customer service. A measurable criterion might be making sure the customers receive exactly what they order 100 percent of the time. By using numbers to clarify amount and time, you know what to shoot for.

In some cases, you need to do more than increase your awareness of expected standards. If your work quality is substandard, look for an underlying cause. Ensure that you have the skills and knowledge you need to complete a task. Sometimes you can't complete work to a high standard without developing additional skills. Substandard work may stem from other causes as well: boredom, distraction, illness, stress, conflict, disorganization, or procrastination. Use your problem-solving skills from Chapter 8 to determine the cause and find a solution.

Set your own standards

Top-performing workers not only meet but also exceed standards and expectations. Their personal standards are higher than the accepted standards set by others. They take on additional responsibilities and are resourceful in finding ways to get the work done effectively. These are exceptional workers.

What motivates people to exceed standards and expectations? Perhaps they find it easy to achieve the accepted performance standards. In this case, workers may exceed expectations just to keep busy. Workplace standards should challenge employees; otherwise, over time, workers may become bored and dissatisfied with their roles. Ideally, work expectations should be achievable with effort. As individuals master tasks and roles, they can take on additional responsibilities and meet higher standards.

Over time, supervisors and employees should review, discuss, and adjust expectations to reflect employees' ongoing learning and development. Workers may reach a point at which they are unlikely to improve their results. This can happen when they are working to full capacity or have little time to develop and grow. Some people are satisfied working at this level, but others gradually may lose interest if the work does not provide additional challenges and opportunities for development. Is your work challenging? If not, you may need to set and achieve higher standards.

When setting standards, consider the following questions

- What does top performance look like?
- How do you define and measure it?
- Are you currently achieving that standard?
- What can you do to meet the standard?

After you define a high standard of performance, you can start to improve your work. Pick a role model—an expert in your field who has achieved similar goals or is highly competent and accomplished. Pay attention to his or her behavior and mirror those actions in your work. Ask your role model to mentor you or provide feedback.

Be aware that some long-term employees are complacent and unmotivated. They may tell new workers, "Slow down, you are making us look bad." This practice discourages high performance. Some people "serve time" until they can retire or afford to leave the organization. You may have heard them counting the years, months, hours, or even seconds until their release. Others watch the clock to ensure that they do not spend a minute more than their required time on the job. If you are watching the clock rather than achieving results, you are just putting in hours. Coworkers and supervisors will notice this behavior, and they will not think of you for promotions, projects, or referrals.

Because you are reading this book, it is doubtful you take a time-watching approach to work. If you do, perhaps you are in the wrong kind of work. If you want to foster career success, exceed expectations by focusing on achieving results rather than simply putting in hours. Plan to complete a task before you take a break or go home for the day. Help out if there is a temporary rush or spike in work volume.

At the same time, balance achievement with self-care. Sometimes you may set overly high expectations for yourself. This can lead to stress and burnout. If you strive for perfection in all of your efforts, your unrealistic expectations may interfere with your career success. Learn to accept less-than-perfect results while maintaining realistic performance standards.

If you have trouble achieving expected results, use your problem-solving skills to identify reasons for your difficulty. Perhaps you aren't prioritizing, planning, and organizing efficiently or communicating or managing information effectively. For example, maybe you failed to complete a report because you could not find the necessary information, or didn't close a deal because you lack the communication skills to develop rapport and listen to customer needs. After you identify what is causing your difficulty, address the problem directly.

Are You Continuously Improving?

Top-performing workers always continue to improve their effectiveness. While consistently achieving high standards, they also streamline their work methods. You have already learned about the importance of prioritizing, planning, and organizing time and tasks to improve your effectiveness. Directly analyzing your work roles and performance can also help you improve your effectiveness. It enables you to set standards and achieve results as well as exceed expectations by continually learning and improving.

See if you continuously improve your work performance by checking the statements describing your work standards. If you check off statements in the first list, look for ways to minimize these behaviors and strive to operate in the continuous improvement mode.

Working to minimal accepted standards without improving processes

- ☐ I complete work the way it has always been done
- ☐ I don't look for opportunities to improve results
- ☐ I set minimal work standards
- ☐ I use statements such as "That's good enough to get by"

Continually improving work processes and exceeding standards

- ☐ I analyze how the work is being done
- ☐ I find ways to improve results
- ☐ I set standards higher than I'm expected to
- ☐ I implement changes to improve results

You might argue that those who achieve excellent results don't need to analyze and improve their work process. Companies do benefit from having workers who consistently accomplish goals. However, the world of work is changing so fast—with new equipment, situations, markets, and competitors turning up every day—that companies can only thrive if work processes evolve with the times.

Success Story: Drowning in Paper

A human resources assistant was responsible for collecting resumes for advertised positions. Her standard procedure was to print out all of the resumes and then give a copy to the human resources team. This practice worked well when a small number of candidates applied for each position. But as the number of applicants increased, the process became inefficient both for her and for the hiring team. Together they set up a list of criteria for each position. She scanned the resumes and printed only those that met the criteria. Her team greatly appreciated her initiative; they saved considerable time and resources by reviewing only the resumes of qualified applicants.

Improving results

Start by evaluating your process for achieving results. You may be so focused on your daily tasks that you never take time to think about your work habits. Yet a few changes might make you much more effective. Look first at the short-term, practical aspects of your work. Challenge yourself to find ways to complete tasks faster and with less effort. Focus on the quality, timeliness, and usefulness of what you do. Compare current tasks with other projects you or others have done well. Here are some questions to stimulate your thinking in this area.

- How can I do the work more efficiently?
- Am I doing my tasks in the best order?
- Do I spend time waiting for anything? Can I avoid waiting?
- Am I repeating tasks rather than doing them right the first time?
- Did I anticipate problems and plan how to handle them?
- Can I streamline any tasks?
- Can I omit any tasks without producing substandard work?
- Is the equipment I need to use well maintained?

As well as looking at short-term, immediate ways to improve a process, you should consider making long-term, broader work improvements. Align your work to the goals of your team, department, or organization. Broad improvements require additional time and energy and may not show immediate results. However, when you improve a frequently used, inefficient work process, you'll reap benefits in the long term. Think about the results you currently achieve through your work. The following questions will stimulate your thinking in this area.

- How do my results benefit the organization?
- Can I find new ways to achieve results?
- How do my results affect other processes in the organization?
- Am I receiving the input I need from others at the best time?
- Might I receive the input I need from others in a better way?
- Am I using the best possible equipment to do this work?
- Am I using the best possible process to do this work?
- Have I set up the physical space to maximize results?
- Can I upgrade my skills or knowledge to achieve better results?
- What can I do to improve my work overall?

Improving processes can also benefit your coworkers and improve workflow. When your work aligns to the work of others, the entire process runs more smoothly. Here are some questions to stimulate thinking in this area.

- Can I improve my results to make them more useful to others?
- Am I delivering results to others at the best time?
- Am I delivering results to others in the best possible way?
- Are others inconvenienced by my work processes?

You can also improve results by taking on additional responsibilities. Expanding work roles enhances your learning and makes you more skilled and marketable. When improving results, look for opportunities to expand and diversify your work roles. Many organizations support self-improvement efforts and expect people to take on additional responsibilities. However, some organizations have highly structured roles and may disapprove of attempts to take initiative and step outside a prescribed set of activities. Understand the norms and expectations of your organization. To expand your roles, you may need to maneuver through roadblocks.

Risk Taking

Everyone is comfortable working on tasks at which they are highly competent. However, this provides few opportunities for learning and improvement. People take risks when they try new ways of achieving results. This risk taking is an essential step for improving your performance. Although you can improve systems and processes incrementally with little risk, significant improvement usually requires trying something completely different. Not everyone is comfortable taking risks. But to be competitive, people and organizations sometimes must rethink the way they do their work.

Not all risk taking is good. Taking appropriate risks is not the same as acting impulsively. Good risk taking is carefully planned. As well, some risks can have far-reaching consequences, both negative and positive. Other risks are smaller and less likely to have dramatic results. When you consider trying new strategies to improve your work performance, carefully assess the possible consequences before you act.

Some organizations accept and even encourage risk-taking. Others discourage it. Assess whether you are more comfortable maintaining the status quo or trying new methods; then think about how that inclination fits with the style of your organization. You may need to step up or tone down your experimentation, depending on the environment and culture of your workplace.

Lack of confidence may prevent you from trying new behaviors. To build confidence, expand on your strengths and find supportive people to offer encouragement and positive feedback. Don't expect to take major risks right away. Focus on incremental change. Start with one small action to test the waters.

Many people are afraid to try something new for fear of negative consequences. When you do take a risk and demonstrate initiative, evaluate your success and capture the learning. Gradually move toward increasing your comfort level. When you try new behaviors, you set the stage for continued growth and career success.

Exceed Expectations: Personality Type Strengths and Challenges

All personality types can exceed expectations. Each personality type has unique strengths and challenges aligned to their natural preferences. Read through the information on your personality type for suggestions specifically tailored to your natural way of working.

Responders (ESTP and ESFP)

Responders like tasks that produce immediate results. You may be less interested in analyzing situations in depth or focusing on long-range outcomes. Try using a longer-term strategic approach to manage your work; you may improve your effectiveness. Responders are easily distracted from work by social interactions and other diversions. Recognize when you are becoming distracted and refocus on your goals. You may prioritize tasks by picking the most interesting and immediate one. Exceed expectations by reflecting on and reordering your priorities. Distinguish the important from the interesting. You are likely willing to take risks in familiar realms. You may be less likely to try something new if the area is outside your experience. To improve your results, build on your natural interest in taking action and adapting.

Explorers (ENTP and ENFP)

Explorers tend to underestimate the time and resources needed to accomplish tasks. As a result, you may promise more than you can accomplish. You also may be tempted to try out unrealistic ideas. In the future, when committing to deadlines or taking on new tasks, look carefully at realities and details. Explorers also may work in bursts of inspiration or leave things to the last minute. You usually are spurred to action by time pressure; leave yourself time near deadlines to accommodate your work style. You look for potential and possibilities, so you are more interested in long-term than short-term results. Exceed expectations by finishing short-term, practical tasks on time. Benefit from your comfort with risks and uncharted territory by trying a new approach to familiar tasks.

Expeditors (ESTJ and ENTJ)

Expeditors take a decisive, logical, and results-oriented approach. You quickly take action to accomplish tasks and achieve goals. You may grow impatient when others are not efficient; in these situations, you sometimes find it easiest to take control and organize everyone to get the job done. Sometimes, others will resist this approach, leading to conflict. Although your goal is to complete the work efficiently, you risk losing others' cooperation and goodwill. Exceed expectations by learning to step back and let others work in their own way. You are comfortable taking risks if you are confident they will lead to greater efficiency and positive results. You're less likely to take risks when you doubt the results and your qualifications to get the job done. In such situations, analyze possible consequences and outcomes to increase your comfort with risk taking.

Contributors (ESFJ and ENFJ)

Contributors value, and are motivated by, completing tasks in a collaborative setting and achieving results that are useful to others. From your perspective, meeting the needs of the people involved is as important as completing the task; work is about relationships and interactions as well as the products or services produced. Ensure that you define and communicate your subjective, interpersonal goals and align them with the needs and work of others. When others are unhappy with the way a project is going, you want to stop to resolve conflicts. This cooperative approach motivates you to achieve results. To exceed expectations, strive to focus less on interpersonal dynamics and more on the task at hand. This will increase efficiency. You are comfortable taking risks and trying new behaviors when you work in a supportive environment.

Assimilators (ISTJ and ISFJ)

Assimilators are persistent and conscientious about completing tasks and goals. You are practical and focus on the realities of situations, and you look for the most expedient way to accomplish goals and meet expectations. You prefer clear and specific outcomes and may be uncomfortable when expectations and standards are not clearly defined. In these situations, challenge yourself to seek clarification. You tend to focus on managing the current situation, so you may need reasons or encouragement to focus on longer-term goals and results. You are comfortable with established methods, so you may hesitate to take risks. Exceed expectations by creating clear standards and increasing your comfort with risk taking. Start by taking small risks and trying new behaviors in familiar environments.

Visionaries (INTJ and INFJ)

Visionaries prefer to conceptualize and organize plans from start to finish. You are most comfortable thinking a project through before you initiate action. You prefer long-term goals and may not focus on short-term results. You aren't motivated by tasks that are routine, detailed, or unrelated to your vision. If you need to do such tasks, find ways to link them to a broader purpose or goal. Also, challenge yourself to set short-term, practical, immediate goals. This will help you manage a situation's immediate demands. You often see alternate ways to accomplish tasks, and you are drawn to taking risks and trying new methods. To exceed expectations, balance this strength while keeping in mind that not all existing procedures and approaches need to be replaced.

Analyzers (ISTP and INTP)

Analyzers are resourceful and tenacious troubleshooters who often try doing things in new ways. Finding a problem's cause or evaluating situations attracts you more than organizing and planning to achieve results systematically. You are comfortable taking risks and enjoy finding ways to improve processes, but you may be too quick to bypass or circumvent the rules. Be sure you understand the reasons for existing rules and practices before you try to improve a process. Show others the logic of your revised strategy and formalize the changes in documents such as operating procedures or policies. Exceed expectations by challenging yourself to follow through before moving on to a new task.

Enhancers (ISFP and INFP)

Enhancers strive to make things easier for the people who are important to them. You like completing your tasks and goals in a workplace that respects people and personal values. You may resist completing any task that does not align with your values. You tend to be more excited about starting tasks than completing them, so you may need encouragement to follow through. This is especially true for tasks or goals you don't consider personally meaningful or beneficial to others. You believe a harmonious and collaborative environment leads to the best results, and you are most motivated to follow through and exceed expectations when everyone works cooperatively. You are less driven to achieve results when others do not appreciate your efforts. You are most motivated to take risks and try new methods when you feel supported and when you believe your efforts will benefit others.

Reflection and Action

This chapter shows why you must exceed expectations to achieve career success. To exceed expectations you must be productive at work, prioritizing, planning, and organizing strategies to accomplish your tasks and meet your goals. You will achieve exceptional results by clarifying expectations, setting high standards, and improving results and processes. Do you exceed expectations? Look at your responses to the checklists in the chapter and think about the suggestions offered. In the area below, write out some steps you can take to improve your ability to exceed expectations.

CHAPTER TEN

Thrive in Uncertainty

O ur world is changing rapidly. If you do not pay attention to change, you may miss valuable opportunities to position yourself for success. People who thrive in uncertainty take a heads-up approach to work, observing patterns and trends and anticipating change. They quickly adjust and develop skills and knowledge to stay ahead of the curve.

When you thrive in uncertainty, people see you as curious, flexible, future-oriented, and versatile. They are confident in your ability to cope with unexpected changes. Adaptable and proactive, you make the most of opportunities when they appear. You create opportunities; you don't simply react to forces outside your control.

In contrast, people who do not thrive in uncertainty seem rigid or overly conservative. They look at situations from a single perspective and respond to new circumstances in old ways. When situations change, they are unprepared; as a result, they struggle to cope with new realities. People who do not thrive in uncertainty can be left behind in our rapidly changing world.

175

Are You Anticipating Change?

You may argue that thriving in uncertainty—unlike more obvious career success strategies such as relating to anyone and exceeding expectations—is not necessary for carrying out day-to-day work activities. However, the world is changing so fast that those who maintain the status quo can easily fall behind. Even jobs and institutions that have remained unchanged for a very long time are suddenly transforming. You need to look ahead to get ahead.

Here is a list of reasons you must learn to thrive in uncertainty.

Anticipating and adjusting to change will

- Increase your awareness of the changes affecting you and your work
- Facilitate your ability to move in the direction you want to go
- Help you avoid surprises so you are not caught unprepared
- Focus your energy for learning and development in the right direction
- Prime you for upcoming opportunities
- Allow you to gather information to develop new processes and methods
- Provide insights that help you accomplish tasks in innovative ways
- Benefit your business by helping you create new results or products
- Help you look forward to, rather than fear, the future

Look for patterns and trends from diverse perspectives

To anticipate changes, seek information and look for patterns and trends. Stay current in your field by researching advances and leading-edge practices and processes. Try to examine and evaluate what you hear, see, experience, and think from different perspectives, keeping an open mind. The following checklist will help you evaluate your ability to use multiple perspectives to view the world. If you check off statements in the first list, look for ways to minimize these behaviors; strive to maximize behaviors from the second list.

Ways in which I focus on reality from a single perspective

- ☐ I argue from a single viewpoint.
- ☐ I see only a narrow range of effects and consequences.

☐ I reference only outdated or biased materials.
☐ I'm unaware of new developments in my field.
☐ I avoid conferences or trade shows.
☐ I ignore current publications.
☐ I don't link news and current events to business implications.

Ways in which I look for patterns and trends from diverse perspectives

☐ I summarize or analyze situations using more than one viewpoint.
☐ I acknowledge diverse effects and consequences.
☐ I seek out multiple sources of new information related to my field.
☐ I explore and discuss cutting-edge developments and new ideas.
☐ I attend relevant conferences and trade shows.
☐ I read current publications.
☐ I track news and current events and discuss their business implications.

This open-minded, future-oriented way of looking at the world is very different from the decisive approach that organizations traditionally reward. People often see a strong point of view as a positive characteristic. When people are firm-minded, they are not easily swayed by other opinions. They "stay the course" and persist until the task is completed. This is a helpful characteristic in some situations, but it has its disadvantages as well.

Sometimes you need a flexible, open mind, especially when new information or changing situations make moving in another direction the wiser choice. When you are open to changing your position or approach, you are better at adapting to new circumstances. When old ways of responding are inappropriate, an open-minded person quickly adapts.

It is not always easy to be open-minded about work matters. Many people are more comfortable dismissing information that does not fit their world view and accepting only information that does fit. However, this approach makes it impossible to anticipate, manage, and thrive in uncertainty. Your challenge is to become more aware of, open to, and accepting of multiple perspectives and alternatives.

If you are strongly invested in your point of view, ask yourself why. Your reasons may be practical, idealistic, logical, or values based. Taking an open-minded approach does not mean you dismiss your natural perspective. The goal is to broaden your point of view by adding new, alternative perspectives.

Success Story: Making the Impossible Happen

A sales representative with ENFP personality type preferences consistently set company sales records. He spent considerable time and energy listening to clients and finding ways to meet their needs and solve their problems. He made the impossible happen by looking at possibilities others might not consider. At first, his supervisor was concerned about the sales representative's approach; the rep did not always follow conventional procedures when making his sales agreements. However, the boss soon saw that his employee's adaptable approach got results when traditional sales methods did not. The sales representative also improved his working arrangements by negotiating flexible working hours to fit his personality type and personal situation.

To accept diverse perspectives, you must be able to tolerate ambiguity and uncertainty. When you view something from many perspectives, there is rarely one right answer. You may feel overwhelmed by situations that you can interpret and act on in more than one way. Although you may prefer choosing one course of action, explore at least one alternative. Exploring alternative actions enhances your ability to deal with change.

Excel Your Way: Tips for Judging (J) and Perceiving (P) types

If you have a preference for Judging (J), you may find uncertainty uncomfortable. It is difficult to plan and structure your time when you do not know what is going to happen next. Anchor yourself by finding some consistency within change and then challenge yourself to become open to options and opportunities.

If you have a preference for Perceiving (P), you may enjoy situations that offer multiple options and outcomes. Use your natural tendency to explore opportunities in changing and uncertain situations.

Think like a futurist

To thrive in uncertainty, you must think like a futurist. Futurists study past and present events to make an educated guess about the future. They are alert to the internal and external forces affecting their work and their company as a whole. The accuracy of their forecasts depends on the breadth and accuracy of their information sources as well as their own biases and interpretations.

Some futurists make predictions using population data—information on how many people live in an area, their age, income, marital status, and so forth. Others use economic data or market trends. Whatever data they use, the concept is the same: learn the trends and make predictions.

Identify which of these information sources are readily available to and most useful in your field of work.

Common sources of information for futurists

- Census data or demographics
- Historical data
- Market data
- Personal experiences
- Others' experiences or ideas
- Surveys
- Reports

Common places for finding trend data

- Conferences and trade shows
- Professional publications
- The Internet
- Interviews
- Newspapers
- Magazines

We face a glut of information and a shortage of knowledge, so information by itself is not always helpful. To be an effective futurist, you must also be able to interpret information. After gathering data, process it by analyzing, evaluating, forming opinions, identifying themes or relationships, and then making predictions.

To start thinking like a futurist, read the following list of global predictions from well-known futurists, all of which have become reality. Ask yourself these questions as you read.

- Is this trend affecting my work? How?
- Does this trend offer me new opportunities?
- Will this trend have any negative effects on the work I am doing?
- What might I do to minimize any negative effects of this trend?
- What new skills do I need to benefit from this trend?

Global Trends

- A worldwide marketplace in which products, capital, technology, and ideas move fluidly and rapidly, as well as an emerging trend for localization and sustainability, with a national or regional focus on producing what the community needs
- Rapid growth in communication technology and integration of electronic, entertainment, communication, financial, and information technology and services
- A technological boom in advanced manufactured materials in areas such as expert computer systems, artificial intelligence, robotics, nanotechnology, and biotechnology
- Niche marketing and increased customization; increased power and influence of specialized consumer groups such as youth and women
- Aging of baby boomers and a growing elderly population as life expectancies increase
- Increased numbers of lifestyle options; some seek a faster pace with speedier services, and others look to slow down, simplify, and find meaning
- Increased numbers of small businesses and self-employed workers; more contract and part-time work options
- Uncertainty related to global economic, political, and environmental instability
- An increase in anxiety and fear as well as an increasing focus on happiness and satisfaction

Trends such as these affect people at all levels, from local to global. To uncover such trends yourself, look for new ideas, new points of view, and scientific and technological breakthroughs related to your work. Don't overwhelm yourself with details, but find ways to make future watching a regular part of your activities. Future watching helps you develop a vision of your future that can guide you in your work, learning, and career development. Predicting the future helps you set goals, make plans, and solve problems.

Here are some tips for increasing your awareness of current trends and future possibilities.

Read, listen, and watch

- Review a variety of media sources.
- Review local, regional, and global news.
- Read nonfiction bestsellers.
- Subscribe to newsletters and association publications.
- Pay attention to trend reports.
- Read in a variety of disciplines.

Relate

- Take note of other people's views.
- Form a strong personal network.
- Join or monitor associations.
- Work with various clubs or groups.
- Attend conventions, conferences, and trade shows.
- Talk to potential customers or employers.
- Visit schools and businesses and ask for information.

Reflect

- Notice your reaction to information.
- Note your assumptions and biases.
- Be aware of your needs, likes, and dislikes.
- Challenge yourself to take in new ideas.
- Use logical thinking to evaluate information.
- Use creative and global thinking to imagine new possibilities.

React

- Volunteer in new areas.
- Try different things.
- Visit new places.

Excel Your Way:
Tips for Sensing (S) and Intuitive (N) types

If you have a preference for Sensing (S), you naturally attend to realities and may find it difficult to focus on future possibilities. Start with the data at hand. Look for patterns in past and current changes. Use this information to predict future patterns.

If you have a preference for Intuition (N), you tend on focus on the future. Making links and seeing possibilities come naturally for you. Find resources that predict far-reaching trends and changes. Make sure you find sufficient data to support trends before you act on them.

Are You Adjusting to Change?

Thinking about the future is not enough; you must also adapt to the changes coming your way. Proactive people take action to improve their current situation and position themselves for anticipated changes. Perhaps the most difficult part of adjusting to change is responding quickly to the unexpected.

You can prepare for the future by anticipating change and being open to multiple perspectives and possibilities. Even so, everyone occasionally is caught off guard by change. In this section you will learn how to accommodate both anticipated and unexpected changes. Review the following lists of ineffective and optimal ways to accommodate to change; think about how they match up to your behaviors.

Responding to new situations in old ways

- Being unable to describe what is needed in times of change
- Staying frozen in denial, anger, or other negative emotions
- Refusing to discuss or deal with work and personal effects of change
- Continuing behavior as if the change had not occurred

Adjusting behavior to accommodate change

- Describing what is needed in times of change
- Acknowledging losses and reactions to losses
- Taking action to deal positively with work and personal effects of change
- Taking action after a change to make it easier to move forward

Dealing with unexpected change

People react to unexpected change in a number of ways. For some people—especially those who are attached to the status quo—it can be devastating. However, a significant change can also bring relief or pleasure. Try to anticipate how you will react to a change by assessing how invested you are in the old ways of doing things.

Success Story: Shifting Gears

An accountant with ISTJ personality type preferences liked and excelled at structured and detailed tasks. After a number of years in her career, she was promoted to chief financial officer. In this position she had to do open-ended, future-oriented, strategic planning. She found she was uncomfortable completing this less structured, conceptual work. To thrive in her new job, she developed a set of steps to help her think strategically. She still prefers the concrete, detailed aspects of her work, but she is now comfortable with and competent at strategic planning.

All change, whether good or bad, entails loss. To thrive in times of transition and uncertainty, you need to recognize and acknowledge your losses. Your reactions to change may include a variety of emotions, thoughts, and defense mechanisms—shock, denial, worry, self-doubt, anger, frustration, sadness, and betrayal. You may also experience positive emotions such as approval, excitement, and relief. As change occurs, take inventory of your thoughts and emotions. You may find it helpful to discuss your feelings or grieve your losses. Accepting and dealing with thoughts and emotions associated with loss will help you move ahead.

After you process your feelings, reflect on how to position yourself post-change. You are facing new circumstances and may not yet see the path that will lead you forward.

The uncertainty may feel uncomfortable, but keep in mind that change also brings personal growth. Manage uncertain times by asking yourself the following questions.

- Where can I find information and support to help me manage this change?
- What can I do to better understand this situation?
- How might this change make my life better?
- How might this change enhance my personal growth?

Asking yourself these kinds of thoughtful questions can help you adapt to change. Taking time to reflect on, and speculate about, what comes next prepares you to move forward. As you adjust to change, you may need to take risks, try new things, or start again. You may need encouragement, coaching, or teaching as you explore and implement ways to adjust. During this transition period, be prepared to experience a range of emotions, including optimism, uncertainty, satisfaction, anxiety, happiness, fear, and excitement.

Excel Your Way:
Tips for Extraverts (E) and Introverts (I)

If you have a preference for Extraversion (E), you naturally seek interactions with others to help you deal with change. You want to take action and are most comfortable when you participate in the change.

If you have a preference for Introversion (I), you naturally seek a chance to take in and think about the information before reacting to it. Give yourself time and space to process change.

People require varying kinds and amounts of information and support to cope with the unexpected. Use the following checklist as a starting point for identifying what you need to thrive in times of change. (Some of the items may be more or less relevant, depending on the circumstances.) When you know what you need, you can ask the right questions and find the best ways to adapt to and embrace the change.

In times of change, I seek

- ☐ Facts and details about the changes
- ☐ A chance to discuss what is happening

☐ A specific role or action to carry out
☐ Time to reflect on or get used to the change
☐ A timeline or structured plan for the change
☐ An understanding of the vision or goal behind the change
☐ Logical reasons for the changes
☐ Opportunities to preserve what is already working
☐ Information on how the change will affect people
☐ Reassurance and emotional support
☐ Options and flexibility

Excel Your Way:
Tips for Thinking (T) and Feeling (F) types

If you have a preference for Thinking (T), find out why the unexpected change is occurring. After you understand the reason behind the change, you can logically analyze the situation and adjust.

If you have a preference for Feeling (F), find out how the unexpected change affects the people involved. Look for ways in which the change makes the situation better for people so you can support and encourage those affected.

Are You Ahead of the Change?

You often cannot control events and circumstances or stop the reorganization and upheaval going on around you. But you *can* anticipate and plan for change and initiate behaviors that will increase your chances of success in the future. To be truly proactive, you need to act before change happens and position yourself for upcoming opportunities. Here are some questions to keep in mind.

- What change is likely to occur soon?
- How will this change affect me?
- Am I prepared?
- What can I do to be more prepared?

To capitalize on opportunities, you need to combine self-development and self-promotion. The next section of this chapter explores self-development and ways to approach change proactively. Chapter 11, Promote Your Progress, discusses self-promotion. The risk-taking tips in Chapter 9, Exceed Expectations, can guide you as you adjust your behaviors and try new methods.

Self-Development

Preparing for change usually requires personal development. People with highly successful careers constantly learn and develop their skills. Chapter 7, Cultivate Your Curiosity, emphasizes the importance of lifelong learning and learning how to learn. This section will help you decide how to position yourself for your optimal future.

Self-development is most effective when it is an ongoing process, aligned both with your personal goals and with trends and changes in the outside world. For example, if your goal is to excel at operating a particular type of equipment, you must be aware of change in the industries that use the equipment. If the equipment is used in only one industry, explore that industry's stability. Look for geographical locations where the industry is well established or growing. Do research to find out what financial, political, and environmental factors may influence work availability.

As well as researching the industry, you should explore the equipment itself. What specialized skills do you need to operate it? How can you get training, and how much does the training cost? Can you transfer the training from this piece of equipment to other kinds of equipment? Does the industry have up-to-date equipment? If not, will companies replace the equipment soon? Will you need new training to operate this equipment? Will your chances of career success increase if you can complete basic mechanical maintenance on the equipment you operate? What is the required maintenance training, and how much does the training cost?

Find out if learning to operate less-specialized types of equipment provides more work options and greater flexibility. Align the information you've gathered with your work and life goals. For example, if you are motivated to spend more time at home with family, research equipment-operating positions that require little travel. All this may sound like a lot of work; you're merely trying to choose an equipment-training program, after all. However, when you make a well-thought-out training decision, you know you're investing your money and time wisely.

Your challenge is to ask the right questions and gather the right information so you can see how realities and trends relate to your work and life goals. Gathering facts and thinking about the future help you anticipate and prepare for changes by developing skills and knowledge.

Success Story: Please Pick Me

A woman with ESFJ personality type preferences greatly enjoyed her administrative work. However, the company she worked for was planning to merge with another, much larger organization, and she might lose her job. When the larger organization introduced a new expert computing system to their workforce, she quickly volunteered for training on the system. Taking the training provided her with a competitive edge and when the merger was finalized, she kept her position. Even if her attempt to stay in the organization had not been successful, the enterprising worker still acquired an additional skill to enhance her marketability.

There are always many things to learn. Carefully consider which learning and development opportunities best help you meet your goals. Look at an enticing career opportunity through the eyes of an employer, contract manager, buyer, or anyone with the authority to hire others. What type of candidate are these people looking for? What skills, knowledge, and experience will the best candidates offer? Are you a good fit for the work? What can you learn to get the job you want?

When deciding what you need to learn, consider whether you are a generalist or a specialist. Generalists tend to know a little about many things, which has both advantages and disadvantages. They can engage in several broad kinds of work and easily move between different work opportunities. However, they may not have the depth of knowledge, skills, or experience to obtain work requiring a highly developed, specific, skill set. Generalists may not be as highly paid as specialists.

Being a specialist also has advantages and disadvantages. Specialists tend to have extensive knowledge of a few topics, which usually limits them to a smaller number of work options. They may be highly paid for their work, especially if few people have their specialized knowledge, skills, and experience. It may be hard for out-of-work specialists to find a new position if their specialized work is not in high demand.

If you are a generalist, develop a moderate depth of skills in several complementary areas. This opens more possibilities and may lead to higher pay. If you are a specialist, try to find more diverse applications for your work. Specialists, even more than generalists, need to focus on the future; changes in specialized fields may greatly affect work options. Staying current on cutting-edge changes in your area of specialty is crucial to your ongoing success.

Consider how you prefer to develop as well as what you need and want to develop. You can gain skills and knowledge in many ways. Some of these are formal and easily recognizable by organizations—courses, workshops, structured mentorship, and on-the-job training programs. Other ways of learning are informal but equally effective—reading, observing, self-teaching through exploration and practice, viewing videos, informal mentorship, and Internet research. If you prefer learning informally, be sure to demonstrate your learning so others recognize your expertise. Use the learning skills you developed in Chapter 7, Cultivate Your Curiosity. By being proactive and preparing for the future, you position yourself for career success.

Thriving in Uncertainty: Personality Type Strengths and Challenges

All personality types can thrive in uncertainty. Every personality type has unique strengths and challenges aligned to their natural preferences. Read through the information on your personality type for suggestions specifically tailored to your natural way of working.

Responders (ESTP and ESFP)

The Responder's greatest strength and biggest weakness, in times of change, is your immediate and practical focus. You adapt in the moment and are especially creative when solving practical problems. When faced with changes, Responders react by being highly flexible, maneuvering, and adapting. When coping with unexpected change, find a practical way forward to capitalize on immediate benefits. You may not focus on future trends and may be less interested in long-term effects than in immediate action. Challenge yourself to look for trends and new ideas. Find ways to link your concrete, immediate actions with long-term results. You may be resistant when you cannot see practical reasons for imposed change or when you are not involved in the change. When change is imposed, find ways to actively participate.

Explorers (ENTP and ENFP)

The Explorer's greatest strength and biggest weakness, in times of change, is that you are already there. You tend to be highly proactive, change oriented, and interested in generating possibilities, seeing trends, and anticipating the future. Jumping in and trying something new and different is more enjoyable than repeating what has already been done. You may enjoy acting as a change agent at work, introducing and promoting new ways. When working to implement change, you may miss important facts, details, and steps in the change process. Seeking a total rather than partial change, you may not be concerned about preserving what still works. Challenge yourself to temper your enthusiasm for change with a respect for lessons learned through past experience. You may resist imposed change that does not fit your view of the future, creates additional structure, or limits freedom of action. In these cases, look for positive long-term outcomes and possibilities in the change.

Expeditors (ESTJ and ENTJ)

The Expeditor's greatest strength and biggest weakness, in times of change, is finding logical reasons for change and getting the job done. You naturally analyze how well tasks are being done and focus on making processes more efficient. Even though you want to implement change quickly, sometimes you should pause to consider options. Otherwise you may miss an opportunity to implement a better, less obvious option. In times of change, you may become impatient dealing with others' emotions. Challenge yourself to look at the personal as well as the logical side of changes. Manage unexpected change by getting involved. Take control and influence the structure and plan of the change.

Contributors (ESFJ and ENFJ)

The Contributor's greatest strength and biggest weakness, in times of change, is becoming personally involved in the situation. When looking at trends, you are interested in changes that increase morale or make the workplace environment more harmonious. For you, change is personal. You want to involve and engage everyone in a positive way and dislike situations in which people are unsure about or uncomfortable with change. Promote change by addressing people's needs and fears. Take time to discuss and deal with personal responses. But be aware that not everyone wants to delve into personal responses; you may need to challenge yourself to find and accept practical, logical reasons for change. Get involved by showing others the benefits of, or by helping them adjust to, the change. Accept the negative consequences of change and move beyond these to find potential benefits for the people involved.

Assimilators (ISTJ and ISFJ)

The Assimilator's greatest strength and biggest weakness, in times of change, is preserving the status quo. You prefer practical, well-thought-out, organized, incremental change. You want to safeguard what works and can be uncomfortable trying something new; you may not trust changes to existing, reliable processes. When managing change, gather information about the specific tasks, timelines, and details of new realities. Take time to reflect, accept, and plan before implementing change. Improve the situation by sharing your experiential knowledge of what will and will not work. At the same time, challenge yourself to let outdated methods go; otherwise, you may fall behind when change occurs. To anticipate change, search past and current data for patterns and extrapolate to predict future trends.

Visionaries (INTJ and INFJ)

In times of change, the Visionary's greatest strength, and biggest weakness, is a focus on the long-term future. You are a natural future-watcher; you are stimulated by anticipating and predicting change. You visualize sweeping global changes, and develop complex, long-range plans for adapting to those changes. However, when change happens, you may get lost in ideas and possibilities and neglect reality. Challenge yourself to pay greater attention to the facts and details of the here and now. Avoid describing change using abstract language and concepts. Although you may find it frustrating to translate your abstract ideas into practical steps, that's the way get others to buy into your vision. Balance your desire to think about and plan for change with your desire to achieve results. When dealing with unexpected change, find additional sources of information and look for the long-term benefits.

Analyzers (ISTP and INTP)

In times of change, the Analyzer's greatest strength, and biggest weakness, is analysis and skepticism. When looking toward the future, you see logical links between actions and consequences. You are willing to adapt as necessary, and you embrace any change that seems reasonable and sensible to you. However, you resist, maneuver around, ignore, or avoid change that strikes you as illogical. When you don't buy into a change, you may grow detached or noncompliant. To become open to change you might naturally oppose, look for the logic behind it. Discover ways in which the change makes things quicker or easier. You may become impatient with highly structured changes that require you to follow many rules and procedures. Manage these situations by finding ways to act independently. Analyze the implications of the change, find options, and negotiate your involvement. Challenge yourself to consider the personal as well as the logical consequences and implications of change.

Enhancers (ISFP and INFP)

In times of change, an Enhancer's greatest strength, and biggest weakness, is a need to see meaning. You are sensitive to, and focused on, the needs of others. So when change comes, you first consider the implications and consequences of change on those around you. You generally adapt well to change when necessary and even embrace change that improves others' situations. However, if change is incongruent with your values, you may become resistant and inflexible. You also may wait to share your concerns until you become frustrated. Challenge yourself to share your concerns early in the change process and to see the logical as well as the personal side of the change. Talk to supportive people to process your opinions and feelings. This will help you move forward with energy and a positive attitude. Find a meaningful part to play in the change process.

Reflection and Action

This chapter shows why it's crucial to be able to thrive in uncertainty. Those who thrive in uncertainty are ready for the future; they pay attention to trends and anticipate change, positioning themselves for success. When surprised by unexpected changes, they quickly reassess their position and adapt to the new realities. Do you have the habits and skills you need to thrive in uncertainty? Look at your responses to the checklists in the chapter and think about the suggestions offered. In the area below, write out some steps you can take to improve your ability to thrive in uncertainty.

CHAPTER ELEVEN

Promote Your Progress

The final career success strategy is self-promotion. It's the key to putting your career in motion, No matter how skilled and conscientious you are, you won't achieve success until you promote yourself. By promoting yourself, you make other people aware of your skills, interests, goals, services, or products; you tell them who you are and what you can do for them.

Self-promotion gives you an opportunity to highlight and capitalize on your strengths. Promoting your unique set of abilities can help you find an optimal position within an organization; it can also put you in line for opportunities and advancements that suit your talents. If self-employment is your goal, you must promote your services or products to find customers. No matter what your situation, if you want to meet your career and life goals you need to display your talents to the world.

Many people are uncomfortable with the idea of promoting themselves and have no idea how to do it. Maybe you are one of them. Perhaps you prefer to stay in the background and find it difficult or embarrassing to talk about yourself and your abilities. You may think your work speaks for itself, and sometimes this is true. But in most cases, you need to draw attention to your talents. If you don't, others won't necessarily recognize your contributions or know what you have to offer. You'll be passed over for opportunities because no one will realize that you are the best person for the job.

Are You Promoting Yourself?

Read the following checklist to determine if you are promoting yourself. Check off the self-promotion strategies you are already using. If you don't check off an item, think of actions you might take to use the strategy. The next section shows you how to become a more effective self-promoter.

☐ Others see my enthusiasm and commitment for developing my career
☐ Others know about my key career goals and objectives
☐ I share my successes and accomplishments with others
☐ Others recognize my skills and knowledge
☐ I make an effort to talk to others and share information about myself
☐ I show samples of my best work to people who could help me advance my career
☐ I seek out opportunities to be recognized for my work
☐ Others are aware of my availability and interest when new opportunities arise

Success Story: Getting in the Door

A woman with ISFP personality type preferences created beautiful pottery. She hoped to establish herself as an artisan in her local area but felt awkward talking with gallery owners to promote her work. So the potter invested considerable effort in practicing her sales pitch with a close friend. She also created a portfolio with pictures of her best pieces. She took her portfolio and three favorite pieces to one gallery owner, and the owner responded positively. She repeated this strategy several times, and her work is now in four different galleries in the city.

Before engaging in self-promotion, recognize and clarify your unique skills, characteristics, and contributions. Use your knowledge of personality type and career success strategies to explore your preferences and strengths. Review your career and life goals and decide what you should share about yourself, and why. What do others need to know to hire or promote you, or otherwise advance your career? Think about your personality traits as well as your specific skills and knowledge. Characteristics such as enthusiasm and initiative are as important as knowledge of particular equipment.

Here are some qualities and accomplishments you might wish to highlight.

Qualities to promote

- Skills
- Experience
- Competence
- Awards
- Achievements
- Interests
- Goals
- Career direction
- Initiative
- Enthusiasm
- Availability
- Ideas
- Commitment

Excel Your Way:
Tips for Sensing (S) and Intuitive (N) types

If you have a preference for Sensing (S), you may find it easier to promote your skills and experience than to promote less tangible personal characteristics and goals. List your experiences, skills, and accomplishments and look for themes in your list. Identifying themes will help you decide what is most important to promote.

If you have a preference for Intuition (N), you may find it easier to promote your goals and dreams than to promote specific skills. Challenge yourself to identify skills and experience that are relevant to your goals. Promote these skills and experiences to achieve career success.

After identifying your strengths, find ways to demonstrate your abilities within your organization. One good way to start is by modeling high performance. If you are consistently enthusiastic and positive, others will notice. Then share examples of your best work, such as websites, work samples, and articles in newsletters or journals. Since not everyone is in a position to observe your accomplishments, you also need to talk about your competencies.

Effective self-promotion must suit the time, place, people, and situation. Don't try to promote yourself at an event held to recognize or celebrate someone else's accomplishments. In such a situation, turning the focus away from the honoree is inappropriate and competitive. Similarly, avoid self-promotion during conversations that are focused on someone or something else. Be tactful and wait for the appropriate opportunity to share your expertise.

Avoid directly comparing yourself to others. For example, don't say, "I could do a much better job than she did." This is counterproductive; you will come across as negative and competitive. A more tactful statement is, "Perhaps we could use a different strategy for accomplishing this. I think it would work to . . . ." This approach allows you to share your expertise without the negative tone.

Excel Your Way: Tips for Extraverted (E) and Introverted (I) types

If you have a preference for Extroversion (E), self-promotion may come easily to you. Your challenge is to limit your self-promotion and make sure you do not monopolize conversations or promote yourself in inappropriate situations.

If you have a preference for Introversion (I), you may hesitate to self-promote, waiting for the right time to speak. Others may underestimate your abilities. Your challenge is to find more opportunities to work self-promotion into a conversation. Practice a few self-promotional phrases to use when the opportunity arises.

How do outstanding individuals in your organization, association, or community receive recognition? They may be written up in newsletters; they may win competitions and accept awards or receive honors in recognition programs. Research how these people are chosen for recognition. They may have nominated themselves, or they may have been nominated by others. If you contributed or achieved in an area for which one of these individuals is being recognized, enter the competition or recognition program. Public recognition is a valuable self-promotion tool. If your achievements are acknowledged in an organizational setting, you will become more recognizable throughout the company.

Success Story: Getting Recognition

Two partners ran a small consulting business. They completed innovative projects and wanted to let the community know about their services. They learned about a "small business of the year" competition in their city. After studying the criteria for the reward, they decided to enter the competition. They put substantial effort into the process, filling out application forms, writing a business description, and providing client references and letters of recommendation. Their effort paid off: They won. At the award ceremony, they networked and built connections with community members. Winning the award brought their consulting business free publicity from local newspapers and television stations. The partners also mentioned the award on their résumés, in their portfolios, and in other promotional materials.

Although highlighting your work is a great starting point, the real power of self-promotion is in talking to people. Build a broad network, as described in Chapter 6. Relate to anyone. Start by promoting yourself to your closest contacts. This is less threatening than talking to acquaintances or business connections. Then join associations and attend networking events and work functions. Let others know who you are and what you want to do. Find opportunities to share your successes, and let others know about your career goals. Ask them for advice, ideas, and contacts that can help promote your career.

You can promote yourself in almost any type of conversation. Be brief, focused, and tactful. To prepare yourself, create some short promotional statements to use in conversations. Describe brief examples of your accomplishments or mention your interest in certain activities. Share a snapshot of your goals.

For example, imagine you wrote a set of procedures for your organization and are interested in writing more. In conversation with your organization's leader, you may have the opportunity to say, "You might find it helpful to look at the procedures I wrote for that task. I tried to make them as clear and specific as possible. Let me know what you think." These statements point out the work you did and open the door for the leader to review it. Later, you might say that you enjoy writing procedures and inquire about upcoming writing projects. These statements demonstrate your interest and availability.

Seek feedback from others; ask them whether you use self-promotion appropriately. If not, refine your approach. You should always be tactful, making sure your assets are recognized without coming across as arrogant or overconfident. Avoid overplaying your abilities or being too quick to self-promote. If you sense you are overpromoting yourself, turn the conversation toward the interests and accomplishments of others. Your goal may be self-promotion, but you still need to demonstrate empathy and listening skills. (Review Chapter 5, Learn from Everyone, if you need a refresher.) Make sure others know you are listening to and understand their point of view.

Success Story: Sharing the Spotlight

When a counselor with ENFJ personality type preferences moved to a new town, she decided to build a referral network. She asked other counselors about their expertise and shared her special interest areas with them. Whenever clients came to her with needs outside her areas of expertise, she referred them to one of the other counselors. After some time, the other counselors also began to refer clients to her. By discussing and establishing areas of expertise with others, the counselor used self-promotion to create a situation in which everyone benefited.

Excel Your Way:
Tips for Thinking (T) and Feeling (F) types

If you have a preference for Thinking (T), you may assume that your accomplishments are self-evident. Realize others may not be aware of your expertise and challenge yourself to find tactful ways to point out your competencies.

If you have a preference for Feeling (F), you may believe it is arrogant to discuss your accomplishments. Your challenge is to engage in more direct and assertive self-promotion.

When you have mastered all ten career success strategies outlined in this book, you will be primed for success. You will know what career success looks like and will take personal responsibility for obtaining it. You know how to demonstrate a positive attitude, listen, and communicate effectively. You value learning, have honed your thinking skills, exceed expectations, and thrive in change. When you demonstrate your strengths to others, you'll have the last strategy in place to create your ideal career.

Excel Your Way:
Tips for Judging (J) and Perceiving (P) types

If you have a preference for Judging (J), use your natural decision-making skills to decide on your goals and take action to reach them. Plan what to promote and how to accomplish your self-promotion. Challenge yourself to take advantage of unexpected promotional opportunities.

If you have a preference for Perceiving (P), you may want to seize an opportunity spontaneously rather than plan your self-promotion. Spontaneity is one of your natural strengths, but it cannot replace a more structured effort. Challenge yourself to make a structured plan for self-promotion.

Promoting Your Progress:
Personality Type Strengths
and Challenges

All personality types can promote their progress. Each personality type has unique strengths and challenges aligned to their natural preferences. Read through the information on your personality type for suggestions specifically tailored to your natural way of working.

Responders (ESTP and ESFP)

As a Responder, you can use your active and energetic approach to promote yourself. Your strength is showing rather than telling people what you can do. Quick to respond to unexpected opportunities, you easily promote yourself and demonstrate your progress in the moment. Challenge yourself to make a strategic plan for promoting your career into new roles that aren't likely to occur by happenstance.

Explorers (ENTP and ENFP)

As an Explorer, you like to develop and position yourself for opportunities. You usually are comfortable sharing your enthusiasm and promoting yourself. Because you can envision many possible futures and find it easy to change your career direction, you may tend to promote a wide range of ideas and qualities. But try to focus your self-promotion to some degree; otherwise, other people won't know what matters most to you.

Expeditors (ESTJ and ENTJ)

As an Expeditor, you like to set structured career goals and strive to achieve them. You are comfortable highlighting your strengths and competencies. Be wary of making negative comments about others' abilities and standards; people may take offense at your analytical comparisons. Always use tact when you self-promote.

Contributors (ESFJ and ENFJ)

As a Contributor, you may focus on your work group's achievements and neglect to promote yourself as an individual. You may tend to speak of achievements in terms of "we" rather than "I." Others appreciate this approach, but it won't get you any recognition for your own individual efforts. Work to define and share your unique contributions to team achievements.

Assimilators (ISTJ and ISFJ)

As an Assimilator, you usually do not talk about your achievements unless you are sharing information about an area of expertise. Challenge yourself to initiate more casual conversations. When you describe your expertise, summarize your competencies concisely; otherwise, you may provide so many details that you overwhelm your listeners. You may find it easier to promote yourself when a specific opportunity arises.

Visionaries (INTJ and INFJ)

As a Visionary, you may have many big-picture ideas about your career progress. To promote your vision, translate your ideas into practical, immediate goals to share with others. Challenge yourself to determine the first steps toward your long-term goals and promote qualities that are related to those steps.

Analyzers (ISTP and INTP)

As an Analyzer, you may believe that highlighting your strengths is stating the obvious. Social networking to promote your competencies may seem a waste of time. Challenge yourself to seek networking opportunities and discuss your abilities and career aspirations with others. Initiate conversations with general topics before you move into self-promotion.

Enhancers (ISFP and INFP)

As an Enhancer, you are more comfortable emphasizing others' contributions than promoting your own. Start your self-promotion efforts with people you trust and know well. Challenge yourself to share your aspirations and abilities with a broader range of people. You may find it easier to show samples of your work than to talk about your attributes. Focus on your unique qualities.

Reflection and Action

This chapter shows why promoting your progress is essential. Assess your current efforts for promoting your abilities and career aspirations. Think about the suggestions offered in the chapter. In the area below, write out some steps you can take to promote your progress.

Additional Resources

Barger, N., and Kirby, L. K. *The Challenge of Change in Organizations.* Mountain View, CA: Davies-Black Publishing, 1995.

Bender, P. *Leadership from Within.* Toronto, ON: Stoddart Publishing, 1997.

Berens, L., and Isachsen, O. *A Quick Guide to Working Together with the Sixteen Types.* Huntington Beach, CA: Telos Publications, 1992.

Bolles, R. *What Color Is Your Parachute?* Berkeley, CA: Ten Speed Press, 2008.

Bridges, W. *Managing Transitions: Making the Most of Change* (2nd ed.). New York: Perseus Publishing, 2003.

Campbell, D. P. *If You Don't Know Where You're Going, You'll Probably End Up Somewhere Else.* Notre Dame, IN: Sorin Books, 2007.

Covey, S., Merrill, R., and Merrill, R. *First Things First.* New York: Free Press, 1996.

Davis, M., Robbins Eshelman, M., McKay, M., and Fanning, P. *The Relaxation & Stress Reduction Workbook.* Oakland, CA: New Harbinger Publications, 2008.

De Bono, E. *Six Thinking Hats.* New York: Back Bay Books, 1999.

Dubois, D. *Competency-Based Performance Improvement.* Amherst, MA: HRD Press, 1993.

Dunning, D. *What's Your Type of Career?* Palo Alto, CA: Davies-Black Publishing, 2001.

Dunning, D. *Introduction to Type® and Communication.* Mountain View, CA: CPP, Inc., 2003.

Dunning, D. *Type and Training: Type Practitioner Series.* Mountain View, CA: CPP, Inc., 2007.

Dunning, D. *Introduction to Type® and Learning.* Mountain View, CA: CPP, Inc., 2008.

Fairhurst, A., and Fairhurst, L. *Effective Learning, Effective Teaching.* Mountain View, CA: Davies-Black Publishers, 1995.

Fitzgerald, C., and Kirby, L. K. (Eds.). *Developing Leaders.* Palo Alto, CA: Davies-Black Publishing, 1997.

Gelatt, H. B. *Creative Decision Making Using Positive Uncertainty.* Mississauga, ON: Crisp Learning, 2003.

Hammer, A. L. *Introduction to Type® and Careers.* Mountain View, CA: CPP, Inc., 1993.

Hirsh, S. K., and Kummerow, J. M. *Introduction to Type® in Organizations* (3rd ed.). Palo Alto, CA: CPP, Inc., 1998.

Krebs Hirsh, S., and Kise, J. *Work It Out, Revised Edition: Using Personality Type to Improve Team Performance.* Mountain View, CA: Davies-Black Publishing, 2006.

Kroeger, O., and Thuesen, J. *Type Talk at Work.* New York: Dell Publishing, 1992.

Lawrence, G. *People, Types, and Tiger Stripes.* Gainsville PL: Center for Applications of Psychological Type, 1993.

Long, C. *How to Survive Without a Salary: Learning How to Live the Conserver Lifestyle.* St. Charles, IL: Charles Warwick Publishing, 1996.

Myers, I. B., with Myers, P. B. *Gifts Differing: Understanding Personality Type.* Palo Alto, CA: Davies-Black Publishing, 1995.

Myers, I. B. *Introduction to Type®* (6th ed.). Mountain View, CA: CPP, Inc., 1998.

Myers, I. B., McCaulley, M. H., Quenk, N. L., and Hammer, A. L. *MBTI® Manual: A Guide to the Development and Use of the Myers-Briggs Type Indicator®* (3rd ed.). Palo Alto, CA: CPP, Inc., 1998.

Myers, K. D., and Kirby, L. K. *Introduction to Type® Dynamics and Development: Exploring the Next Level of Type.* Mountain View, CA: CPP, Inc., 1994.

Pearman, R. R., and Albritton, S. C. *I'm Not Crazy, I'm Just Not You.* Mountain View, CA: Davies-Black Publishing, 1997.

Quenk, N. L. *Was That Really Me? How Everyday Stress Brings Out Our Hidden Personality.* Mountain View, CA: Davies-Black Publishing, 2002.

Quenk, N. L. *In the Grip: Understanding Type, Stress, and the Inferior Function.* Mountain View, CA: CPP, Inc., 2000.

Robinson, D., and Robinson, J. *Performance Consulting.* San Francisco: Berrett-Koehler Publishers, 1995.

Schaubhut, N. A., and Thompson, R. C. *MBTI® Type Tables for Occupations.* Mountain View, CA: CPP, Inc., 2008.

Seligman, M. *Learned Optimism: How to Change Your Mind and Your Life.* New York: Random House Inc., 2006.

Thomson, L. *Personality Type: An Owner's Manual.* Boston, MA: Shambhala Publications, 1998.

von Oech, R. *A Whack on the Side of the Head: How You Can Be More Creative.* New York: Business Plus, 2008.

Index

A

Act and Adapt personality type, 12–13
active listening, 68–69, 75
adrenaline, 31
Analyzers: change and, 191; characteristics of, 18–19; communication style of, 104; conflict resolution by, 104; decision making by, 151; exceeding expectations by, 172; feedback style of, 104; learning by, 125; listening style of, 82–83; outlook of, 41; problem solving by, 151; self-promotion by, 201; stress response by, 41; thinking style of, 151; thriving in uncertainty, 191; working style of, 62
anticipating of change, 185–188
asking yourself for directions: career goals, 21–23; description of, 1–2; personality types. *See* personality types; working, 11–20
Assimilators: change and, 190; characteristics of, 16–17; communication style of, 103; conflict resolution by, 103; decision making by, 150–151; exceeding expectations by, 171–172; feedback style of, 103; learning by, 124; outlook of, 40–41; problem solving by, 150–151; self-promotion by, 200; stress response by, 40–41; thinking style of, 150–151; thriving in uncertainty, 190; working style of, 62
association memberships, 109
attention, 55–56
attitude: description of, 25–26; idealistic, 37; optimistic, 27; pessimistic, 27
auditory learners, 116

B

bias, 110, 115
blaming, 45–46, 49
body language, 82–83, 90
boredom, 56–57
brainstorming, 143

C

Care and Connect personality types, 19–20
career goals: family influences on, 22; setting of, 21–23
career success: defining of, 20; measures of, 5; self-assessments, 20–21; strategies for, 1–4
change: adjusting to, 182–185; anticipating of, 176–182, 185–188; reactions to, 183; self-development and, 186–188; unexpected, 183–185
check statements, 71
clarifying expectations, 75–77, 162–164
commitment to work, 36–37
Communicate and Cooperate personality types, 15–16
communication: by Analyzers, 104; by Assimilators, 103; audience of, 90; check statements for, 71; clarifying the purpose